WITHDRAWN

ENGLISH DRAMA

Series Ed...
Bruce King

'E.   'VE

ENGLISH DRAMATISTS
Series Editor: Bruce King

Published titles

ENGLISH DRAMATISTS

WEBSTER AND FORD

Rowland Wymer

Lecturer in English, University of Hull

St. Martin's Press

First published in Great Britain 1995 by
MACMILLAN PRESS LTD
Houndmills, Basingstoke, Hampshire RG21 2XS
and London
Companies and representatives
throughout the world

A catalogue record for this book is available
from the British Library.

ISBN 0–333–56737–4 hardcover
ISBN 0–333–56738–2 paperback

10   9   8   7   6   5   4   3   2   1
04   03   02   01   00   99   98   97   96   95

Printed in Malaysia

First published in the United States of America 1995 by
Scholarly and Reference Division,
ST. MARTIN'S PRESS, INC.,
175 Fifth Avenue,
New York, N.Y. 10010

ISBN 0–312–12455–4

Library of Congress Cataloging-in-Publication Data
Wymer, Rowland.
Webster and Ford / Rowland Wymer.
p.   cm. —(English dramatists)
Includes bibliographical references and index.
ISBN 0–312–12455–4
1. Webster, John, 1580?–1625?—Criticism and interpretation.
2. Ford, John, 1586 (ca.)–1640—Dramatic works. 3. English
drama—17th century—History and criticism. I. Title. II. Series:
English dramatists (St. Martin's Press)
PR3187.W95   1995
822'.309—dc20

94–29877
CIP

For Pauline

Contents

Editor's Preface

Each generation needs to be introduced to the culture and great works of the past and to reinterpret them in its own ways. This series re-examines the important English dramatists of earlier centuries in the light of new information, new interests and new attitudes. The books are written for students, theatre-goers and general readers who want an up-to-date view of the plays and dramatists, with emphasis on drama as theatre and on stage, social and political history. Attention is given to what is known about performance, acting styles, changing interpretations, the stages and theatres of the time and theatre economics. The books will be relevant to those interested in or studying literature, theatre and cultural history.

BRUCE KING

Acknowledgements

I would like to thank Tom McAlindon, James Booth, John Harris, Graham Satchell, Owen Knowles and Angela Leighton for reading portions of this and offering many useful suggestions. I am also grateful to John Hoyles, Neil Sinyard, Roger Luckhurst, Andrew Butler, and students on the 'Tragedy in the Age of Shakespeare' MA course for discussions I have had with them. I have received a great deal of help with my research from the staff of the Brynmor Jones Library, Hull; the Bodleian Library, Oxford; the Shakespeare Institute, Stratford; and the Prints Department of the British Museum. I also feel greatly indebted to the many directors and actors who have been involved in staging the plays of Webster and Ford in recent years. My last debt of thanks is to Pauline for her encouragement and support while I have been writing this book.

Rowland Wymer

1
Revivals, Reputations and the Question of Value

Plays have their fates, not as in their true sense
They're understood, but as the influence
Of idle custom, madly works upon
The dross of many-tongu'd opinion.
(Prologue to *The Fair Maid of the Inn*)

These things are full of horror, full of pity.
(*The Witch of Edmonton*, III. iv. 69)

In April 1945, a few days before the end of the war in Europe, the Haymarket Theatre presented Webster's *The Duchess of Malfi*, with Peggy Ashcroft as the Duchess, John Gielgud as Ferdinand, and Cecil Trouncer as Bosola. The Victorian confidence in European civilisation and progress, which had made the extreme incidents and behaviour encountered in Jacobean tragedy seem remote and barbarous, had been severely damaged by the First World War and now shattered completely by the atrocities of the Second. No one would now raise the old objection that 'people do not do such things'.[1] *The Times* review appeared under five photographs of the concentration camps just liberated by allied troops. Rather than merely commending the director George

1

Rylands and his cast for a gallant stab at a notoriously unperformable play, critics were lavish in their praise. Edmund Wilson called it simply 'one of the best productions that I have ever seen of anything anywhere'.[2] It had probably been the first completely successful production of a tragedy by Webster or Ford since the Restoration.

Both Webster and Ford were commercial dramatists who did their share of the routine writing necessary to satisfy the seventeenth-century London theatre's incessant demand for new plays. Both collaborated with professionals like Dekker on a number of undistinguished works, yet both also had self-consciously 'literary' ambitions to succeed in the most difficult, demanding and prestigious of dramatic forms – tragedy. Unlike that of Shakespeare, the current critical reputation of both authors is based on a very small number of their plays (all of them tragedies or near-tragedies) and even these have had an erratic stage history. This inevitably provokes a number of questions. Why do we value so highly these particular non-Shakespearean plays above many others that have survived from the period, and are we right to do so? Why does their critical reputation not correlate more closely with their stage history? What factors help to promote successful revivals of these and other Renaissance plays?

Although the history of Shakespeare's reputation is a complex one, with different plays being valued at different times for different reasons, it shows a continuity of both critical esteem and stage performance unmatched by any of his contemporaries (or anyone else, for that matter). Even when not necessarily regarded as England's best dramatist, as in the century or so after his death, he was never seen as less than very important and a core of his plays continued to be performed. Along with Jonson and 'Beaumont and Fletcher', his works had achieved the dignity of a collected Folio edition, and this 'triumvirate of wit' remained critically and theatrically dominant during the remainder of the seventeenth century. The fortunes of Webster and Ford, like those of Marlowe and Middleton, were more varied. The rather skimpy evidence suggests that *The White Devil,*

The Duchess of Malfi and *'Tis Pity She's a Whore*, the three plays most likely to be performed today, probably remained in repertory right up until the closing of the theatres in 1642 and had a sufficiently high reputation to be among the first plays revived at the Restoration. There are records of more than one Restoration performance for all three plays, with *The Duchess of Malfi* scoring a particular success in 1662. John Downes wrote that 'it was so exceedingly excellently acted in all parts, chiefly Duke Ferdinand and Bosola, it filled the house eight days successively, proving one of the best stock tragedies'.[3]

There were other small signs of a continuing enthusiasm for Webster, in particular. John Cotgrave's *English Treasury of Wit and Language* (1655), which collected memorable extracts from about 250 plays, made surprisingly heavy use of Webster – *The Duchess of Malfi* and *The White Devil* being respectively the third and fourth most quoted plays. The fact that the two most extensively quoted plays were Fulke Greville's unperformed political tragedies *Alaham* and *Mustapha* indicates that it was the moral and political weightiness of Webster's dramas which recommended them to Cotgrave rather than their theatrical merits. Samuel Sheppard's *Epigrams* (1651) contained a poem enthusiastically praising *The White Devil* and Sheppard also left an unpublished manuscript, *The Fairy King* (written between 1648 and 1654 and imitating Spenser), one episode of which has Webster being enrolled into a literary 'Hall of Fame', along with twenty-three other English writers. Addressing Webster as a 'Most sacred spirit' (though admitting that 'some may say I dote'), Sheppard tells him:

> Of thy three noble tragedies be as proud
> As great voluminous Jonson; thou shalt be
> Read longer and with more applause than he.[4]

The combination of slight defensiveness ('some may say I dote') with aggressive adulation (placing Webster unambiguously above the more 'voluminous' and critically respected Jonson) is typical of a 'cult' enthusiasm and anticipates the tone of many more recent admirers of Webster. Interestingly, Sheppard (writing during the Commonwealth period) seems certain that

Webster will survive as literature to be 'read', whether or not his plays are actually performed.

The surge of post-Restoration revivals died away as more new plays became available and both the sentiments and language of the earlier drama came to seem forced and extreme. The eighteenth century saw the virtual disappearance from the stage of all Renaissance plays barring those of Shakespeare, Fletcher and Jonson, the one interesting exception being Massinger's *A New Way to Pay Old Debts* in which the part of Sir Giles Overreach provided a star vehicle. Marlowe was never performed and Webster was not staged after 1707, apart from two performances in 1733 of *The Fatal Secret*, adapted by Theobald from *The Duchess of Malfi* but bearing very little resemblance to the original (among other alterations, the Duchess survives and is reunited with Antonio). The only two known revivals of Ford's plays owed nothing to a general renewal of interest in his work but were the product of exceptional circumstances. The second Jacobite rebellion of 1745 occasioned a production of *Perkin Warbeck*, its story of a royal pretender now newly topical. Three years later, the actor Charles Macklin attempted to make some money by staging *The Lover's Melancholy* in conjunction with the publication of forged material apparently indicating that the play was by Shakespeare. Critical interest in Ford, Webster, Marlowe, Middleton, Marston and others was largely confined to scholars seeking to learn more about the context within which Shakespeare had worked.

The decisive landmark in both signalling and helping to effect a change of taste was the publication in 1808 of Charles Lamb's *Specimens of English Dramatic Poets*. Unlike previous anthologies such as Cotgrave's, or Thomas Hayward's *The British Muse* (1738; republished in 1777 as *Beauties of the English Drama*), Lamb chose as far as possible 'to give entire scenes, and in some instances successive scenes, rather than to string together single passages and detached beauties'.[5] His Preface emphasises the emotional power and interest of the plays, expressing the sort of Romantic taste which will reorder the canon and elevate Webster, Ford and Marlowe above Jonson, Fletcher and Massinger:

> The kind of extracts which I have sought after have been, not so much passages of wit and humour, though the old plays

are rich in such, as scenes of passion, sometimes of the deepest quality, interesting situations, serious descriptions, that which is more nearly allied to poetry than to wit, and to tragic rather than comic poetry.[6]

Like other Romantic critics, Lamb thought that Shakespeare's plays were better read than acted and his *Selections* has been accused of being based on literary rather than dramatic criteria. But his decision to print scenes rather than individual passages showed a proper concern to exhibit characters in action and his bias towards the tragic, the poetic and the emotional is replicated in many twentieth-century accounts of which plays really matter.

Hazlitt also celebrated the emotional power of these nearly forgotten plays in his *Lectures on the Dramatic Literature of the Age of Elizabeth* (1819), though he ranked Ford much lower than Lamb had done. He went on to use Webster to attack the failings of modern (that is, Byronic) tragedy which, according to him, gave us only 'the subtleties of the head, instead of the workings of the heart'.[7] Swinburne who, like Hazlitt, placed Webster second only to Shakespeare, praised the 'force of hand, the fire of heart, the fervour of pity, the sympathy of passion' which could be found equally in both.[8] Havelock Ellis's tribute to Ford as an artist 'of the naked human soul' comparable to Stendhal and Flaubert was simply a more modern-sounding version of Lamb's original claim that Ford 'sought for sublimity, not by parcels in metaphors or visible images, but directly where she has her full residence in the heart of man'.[9] These Romantic tributes were to be quoted on playbills and used to justify the first theatrical revivals of a number of non-Shakespearean plays.

By the end of the nineteenth century, a partial critical revolution had been effected. The dramatists which the eighteenth century had neglected were now particularly valued by *fin-de-siècle* aesthetes and decadents, 'the last Romantics', who found in the extreme situations and extreme emotions of the plays of Webster, Tourneur and Ford a challenge to Victorian moral values. This challenge could take the form of a Romantic assertion of a 'higher' morality, as in Swinburne's defiant claim that 'there is no poet morally nobler than Webster', or express itself as a self-consciously 'decadent' relish for the scandalous and the transgressive. There was a recent echo of this second attitude in

the advertising which accompanied the video release of the 1973
Italian film of *'Tis Pity She's a Whore*: 'Dedicated to the macabre,
depraved world of the bizarre, *Redemption Films* brings you a
cocktail of horror, passion and extreme decadence on video . . .
Corrupt yourself now!' The video of *'Tis Pity* appeared in the
centre of the advertisement, flanked by *Killer Nun* and *Salon
Kitty*.[10]

The critical conflict at the close of the century was not only
between orthodox moralists and decadents; it was between those
who wanted to claim that the 'minor' Elizabethans were good
dramatists and those who would concede only that they were
good poets. William Archer, a dramatist himself and an admirer
of Shaw and Ibsen, made use of the rather odd argument that
poetry was 'eternal' whereas drama was 'a thing of convention,
of fashion' to attack Lamb for confusing poetic with dramatic
merit. His conclusion about Webster was that he 'was not, in the
special sense of the word, a great dramatist, but was a great poet
who wrote haphazard dramatic or melodramatic romances for
an eagerly receptive but barbarous public'.[11] This conclusion was
echoed by many other critics, including Edmund Gosse who
called *The Duchess of Malfi* 'pre-eminently a tragic poem to be
enjoyed in the study'.[12]

Archer's comments had been made after seeing William Poel's
1892 production of *The Duchess*, the first of a number of semi-pro-
fessional revivals which self-consciously attempted to re-create
Elizabethan forms of staging. Prior to that, the only nineteenth-
century performances of any plays by Webster or Ford had been
adapted versions of *The Duchess of Malfi*, played as barn-storming
melodrama, which had pleased audiences without convincing
critics that Webster's play was anything more than a 'curiosity'.
Poel's production was let down by indifferent acting and paradoxically its antiquarian 'purism' may have produced something
further removed from Webster's original theatrical appeal than
the less scholarly adaptations, played with all stops out and with
a good performer in the central role. Up till the Second World
War, most non-Shakespearean Renaissance plays could only be
seen in specialist performances put on by groups like Poel's
Elizabethan Stage Society or Allen Wade's Phoenix Society,
founded in 1919. Poel staged *The Broken Heart* in 1898 and the
Phoenix Society put on both *The Duchess* and *'Tis Pity*, but an air

of academic experiment must have hung over many of these productions. Only when top professional companies were prepared
to commit themselves wholeheartedly to making these plays
work before a paying audience would there be a fair test of how
valid were the criticisms made by Archer, Shaw, and others. The
first genuinely public performance of *'Tis Pity* since the seventeenth century was not until 1940.

The successor to Swinburne as a major poet-critic with a particular interest in Shakespeare's contemporaries was of course
T. S. Eliot. Eliot's approach to these dramatists seems to involve
both a continuation of Romantic enthusiasms and a reaction
against them. When – speaking of Shakespeare, Donne, Webster
and Tourneur – he says, 'Their words have often a network of
tentacular roots reaching down to the deepest terrors and
desires',[13] we hear an authentic echo of Swinburne, but Eliot
combines the celebration of intensities of feeling with a modernist emphasis on wit, irony, variety of tone, and linguistic texture.
Despite blaming Lamb for encouraging the distinction between
literature and drama which had set Swinburne and Archer
against each other, Eliot tends himself to approach the plays primarily as poetry and is much better at responding to metrical
nuances and striking figures of speech than at visualising how
scenes might actually work in the theatre. Nevertheless, no one
person was more responsible for creating the kind of taste which
would install Shakespeare's fellow dramatists firmly on university syllabuses and create the audiences which would justify the
mounting of professional productions. Eliot's favoured playwrights – Webster, Middleton, Marlowe, Jonson and Tourneur
(thought to be the author of *The Revenger's Tragedy*) – are still the
ones which dominate academic curricula, while Fletcher and
Massinger languish unread. In coming to accept *The Waste Land*
as the greatest poem of the twentieth century, readers and critics
were also, it could be argued, accepting Eliot's view of the kinship between those Jacobeans whose voices haunt the poem and
modern sensibility. This sense of kinship has not weakened in the
years which have followed, despite the charges of 'incoherence'
and 'decadence' regularly levelled at Webster and Ford (though
not at Middleton and 'Tourneur') by Leavisite critics from the
1930s onwards, charges which have been institutionalised
through their repetition in successive editions of *The Pelican*

Guide to English Literature. Nor have those critical approaches which insist on the historically specific 'otherness' of Renaissance drama inhibited the vigorous life these plays enjoy in the modern theatre.

For a variety of reasons, the plays of many of Shakespeare's contemporaries are now more 'alive', more often performed, more fully appreciated than at any time since the seventeenth century. The last thirty years have been something of a Golden Age in terms of first-class professional productions. There are specific institutional reasons for this as well as less easily defined cultural ones. The expansion of higher education since the war has clearly created a large body of people whose interest in Shakespeare's contemporaries was first stimulated at university. In 1919, Eliot had written with cultivated understatement that Jonson had qualities 'which ought to attract about three thousand people in London and elsewhere'.[14] Even a pessimistic estimate of the present audience for Jonson would want to multiply that figure by at least a hundred. The subsidising of theatres has allowed major companies to risk staging relatively unfamiliar plays and the success of many of these performances, such as the Royal Shakespeare Company's famous 1966 production of *The Revenger's Tragedy*, has helped to expand the stock repertory, increasing the number of plays which have become well known enough to be staged on a normal commercial basis.[15] No recent development has been more important than the opening of the Swan Theatre at Stratford in 1986, which has enabled the RSC to mount a series of superb productions of non-Shakespearean plays in a venue that re-creates the electric proximity of actors to audience which existed in seventeenth-century indoor theatres. The story of the building of the Swan exemplifies some of the contingencies of cultural history since the whole venture was only made possible through the personal generosity of an American millionaire, Mr Fred Koch.

The RSC's policy of having frequent revivals of non-Shakespearean plays was first adopted in the 1960s and it owed much to the perceived affinities between Renaissance drama and forms of contemporary theatre. Particularly influential was Peter Brook's interest in Artaud's dramatic theories which led to the 'Theatre of Cruelty' experiments of the early 1960s. The disturbing but not conventionally tragic combination of black comedy and horror in Peter Weiss's *Marat/Sade* of 1964 provided the appropriate context for an effective revival of *The Jew of Malta*. Trevor Nunn's *Revenger's Tragedy* of two years later was also a product of this interest in Artaud and in modern black comedies like those of Joe Orton. Artaud had in fact singled out the transgressive intensity of *'Tis Pity She's a Whore* for special praise, and the staging of certain scenes in *The Duchess of Malfi*, notably the appearance of the madmen, was influenced for years by the experience of the *Marat/Sade*. A 1967 Italian production of *The Changeling* took this influence to its extreme by turning the main plot into a performance staged in a lunatic asylum by the madmen of the sub-plot.

The importance of many of these plays for post-war directors, as for Eliot earlier in the century, lay in their form and style as much as their content. Their non-realist disruptions of tone and mood permitted the expression of a more varied and sardonic sensibility than that which was recognised by Romantic critics. Tony Richardson gave as one of his reasons for reviving *The Changeling* in 1961 the fact that 'there is a curious and ironic mixture of styles within the play, of abrupt switches from farce to thriller, from thriller to tragedy which to me is very much in tone with contemporary attitudes to writing and in the other arts – a sort of super Hitchcock if you like'.[16] Webster undoubtedly benefited more than Ford from this 'modernist' approach but the preoccupation of both writers with extremes of human behaviour was now an asset rather than a liability in a culture still pondering the implications of Auschwitz and in the process of revaluing *King Lear* as Shakespeare's greatest work. However, like *Lear*, the major plays of Webster and Ford remain too close to a tragic 'norm' to be completely assimilated to modern notions of black comedy or the non-cathartic horror of the 'Theatre of Cruelty'. In the remainder of this chapter I want to give a rather different account of the special value to be found in these plays and why they continue to justify revival.

The Romantic critics, despite their impressionism, ignorance of Elizabethan theatrical practice, and lack of interest in irony and satire, often came closer to conveying the real power of these tragedies than many more recent academic writers. Their emphasis on the affective dimension accords with classical and Renaissance theories of tragedy as a form characterised by its emotional intensity. It also accords with more general Renaissance views about the nature and value of theatrical experience. Dekker's Prologue to *If This Be Not a Good Play, the Devil Is in It*, the play which immediately preceded *The White Devil* at the Red Bull theatre in 1612, resembles Plato's *Ion* in the description it gives of the emotional current which passes from the Muses to the writer, from the writer to the performer, and from the performer to the audience:

> That Man give mee; whose Brest fill'd by the *Muses*,
> With Raptures, Into a second, them infuses:
> Can give an Actor, Sorrow, Rage, Joy, Passion,
> Whilst hee againe (by self-same Agitation)
> Commands the *Hearers*, sometimes drawing out *Teares*,
> Then smiles, and fills them both with *Hopes* and *Feares*.

The White Devil, *The Duchess of Malfi* and *'Tis Pity She's a Whore* are supremely disturbing plays, making immense emotional demands on their audiences. They can modulate swiftly through presentments of sorrow, rage, joy and passion, to compel responses of horror and pity, annihilating any 'safe' distance between the spectator and the actors, in the same way that the Duchess herself is menaced by the madmen who perform before her. Modern academic criticism, in its concern with meaning and contextualisation, has often given an inadequate account of the experience provided by works of art like these. The most famous complaint about this was Susan Sontag's 1964 essay 'Against Interpretation', which finished by saying that 'the function of criticism should be to show *how [a work of art] is what it is*, even *that it is what it is*, rather than to show *what it means*. . . . In place of a hermeneutics we need an erotics of art.'[17]

A more recent version of the same argument, with a more direct application to Renaissance drama, can be found in Norman Rabkin's *Shakespeare and the Problem of Meaning* (1981). After surveying various 'readings' of *The Merchant of Venice*, Rabkin writes that, 'We have been betrayed by a bias toward what can be set out in rational argument.'[18] The desire to draw everything into a coherent and self-contained thesis has resulted in a 'consistent suppression of the nature of aesthetic experience':

The eddying signals communicated by a play arouse a total and complex involvement of our intellect, our moral sensibility, our need to complete incomplete patterns and answer questions, our longing to judge, and that involvement is so incessantly in motion that to pin it down to a 'meaning' is to negate its very essence.[19]

Rabkin says in conclusion that,

The challenge to criticism, I have been suggesting, is . . . to consider the play as a dynamic interaction between artist and audience, to learn to talk about the process of our involvement rather than our considered view after the aesthetic event.[20]

In fact, a good deal of criticism published in the 1980s did express its dissatisfaction with overly neat thematic interpretations premised on the formal and moral coherence of plays, interpretations which had often done particular injustice to Webster. However, it expressed this dissatisfaction not by rising to the challenge of giving a more faithful account of the complex feelings aroused, but by retreating into highly theoretical justifications of formal 'incoherence' which wandered further and further from the experience of these plays in the theatre.

One of the most important and superficially plausible of these critical developments has been the adaptation of Brechtian ideas by Marxist critics of Renaissance tragedy like Jonathan Dollimore. In *Radical Tragedy*, Dollimore follows Brecht in seeing the non-naturalistic discontinuities of style in Jacobean tragedy as a means of alienating the audience from the characters, cancelling the possibilities of empathetic identification and leading to a more critical and politically constructive detachment. However, it is a fallacy automatically to equate realism with emotional identification and non-realistic effects with an intellectual and critical attitude. There is also a false and damaging dissociation of sensibility involved in separating out emotion and understanding into mutually exclusive opposites. For Aristotle, the emotional aspect of tragedy had a cognitive dimension and rather than justice being 'too important to be trusted to empathy',[21] the emotions of pity and terror are closely connected to the development of a sense of *injustice*. Amnesty International advertisements have frequently made the point that people are far more likely to join their organisation in response to the spectacle of human pain than out of abstract principle. Despite *Radical Tragedy* being a substantial book of over 300 pages, Dollimore carefully avoids any extended discussion of *The Duchess of Malfi* since his thesis would not survive a close encounter with it. Brecht's own adaptation of *The Duchess*, first staged in America in 1946, received a belated English première in 1993 and proved to be a thin and impoverished piece of theatre compared with the original, leaving one reviewer 'wondering why Brecht took the project on, since he seems to miss the whole point of the genre'.[22] Ben Jonson, with his constant insistence that his audience become 'judges', anticipates Brecht's particular theatrical strengths far better than writers of tragedy like Webster and Ford.

The self-consciously Brechtian spectator of a tragedy has in fact chosen a rather safe place to sit. Susan Sontag wrote that 'Real art has the capacity to make us nervous',[23] but the Brechtian critic remains in a position of mastery, unthreatened emotionally by the events on stage, unwilling to risk being moved. The rationalist distrust of tragic emotion goes all the way back to Plato, but against it can be set a different kind of aesthetic, one which sees moral change and emotional vulnerability as closely connected. The terror and pity of tragedy go beyond what can be represented and understood in purely rational terms. 'Theatre can only happen the moment the inconceivable really begins' wrote Artaud, whose theories are capable of conveying at least some of the effect of Webster's and Ford's plays.[24] The 'infinitely terrible' death of Brachiano, the horrors of Act IV of *The Duchess of Malfi*, the appearance of Giovanni with his sister's heart impaled on his dagger, take us, in the words of *The Four Quartets*, 'behind the assurance / Of recorded history', back towards 'the primitive terror'. The psychological significance of this sort of spectacle has been discussed by Julia Kristeva in *Powers of Horror* and its justification can be found in our periodic need to re-encounter, in controlled conditions, all that we have repressed or cast out of ourselves in order to achieve identity. However, the full moral and social value of such encounters is more difficult to assert in the absence of Aristotle's other tragic emotion – pity, the missing element in Artaud.

Peter Brook's 'Theatre of Cruelty' experiments were premised on the notion that pity was a comfortable rather than a disturbing emotion:

> A play is not there to 'move' people, that is a ghastly idea. . . . You cry, you have a bath of sentiment, you come out saying you've had a lovely time, but you've had an emotional outlet which has left you complacent. . . . I prefer the notion of disturbance, which leaves you in a greater state of inquiry.[25]

This position clearly has some resemblance to the traditional Marxist suspicion of pity and other 'bourgeois' virtues as ameliorations which help to prevent more radical reforms of social and institutional evils. Against the innocent directness of 'For Mercy has a human heart / Pity, a human face', the Marxist argues, along with Blake's insidious other voice, that,

> Pity would be no more,
> If we did not make somebody Poor:
> And Mercy no more could be,
> If all were as happy as we.[26]

Yet the notion of a world purged entirely of suffering is an absurdity and purely rationalist forms of ethics now appear intellectually bankrupt.

Powerful philosophic support for the idea that tragedy's special value comes from the demand it makes on us to pity suffering, a demand which is far from 'comfortable', can be found in the 'post-rationalist' ethics of the French Jewish thinker, Emmanuel Levinas. For Levinas, the foundations of philosophy lie neither in any possibility of objective knowledge nor in any transcendent subjectivity, but in the inescapably relational character of human existence and the absolute moral demand which the Other makes upon us:

> The other man's death calls me into question, as if, by my possible future indifference, I had become the accomplice of the death to which the other, who cannot see it, is exposed; and as if, even before vowing myself to him, I had to answer for this death of the other, and to accompany the Other in his

mortal solitude. The Other becomes my neighbour precisely through the way the face, summons me, calls for me, begs for me, and in so doing recalls my responsibility, and calls me into question.[27]

Levinas speaks of the pressing proximity of the Other in terms of a 'face to face' relationship and of how 'the face' of the Other makes an 'infinite' demand on us which exceeds any possibility of rationalisation or representation. It is the moral counterpart to the 'infinitely terrible' which tragedy is also capable of suggesting without ever being able fully to represent. It is unclear how far Levinas intends his references to 'the face' of the Other to be taken literally as well as figuratively, but in a theatre the audience and the actors are in a very immediate and literal 'face to face' relationship. This is strongly emphasised in one of the few surviving accounts of an original audience response to the tragedies of Shakespeare and his contemporaries. After watching performances of plays put on by the King's Men at Oxford in 1610 and recalling how their tragedies 'moved the audience to tears', Henry Jackson particularly noted how the dead Desdemona 'entreated the pity of the spectators by her very countenance'.[28] One of the most significant differences between Greek and Renaissance tragedy is that the Greek plays were performed with masks. This would have set limits to the otherwise potentially infinite demands made by the suffering human face.[29] In this connection it is impossible not to think of Ferdinand's reaction to the sight of his murdered sister: 'Cover her face. Mine eyes dazzle: She di'd young.'

Any claim that the emotions aroused by art can have moral value will inevitably have to answer the following question:

Do the identifications with fictions, the inner, tidal motions of pathos and *libido* which the novel, the film, the painting, the symphony unleash within us somehow immunize us against the humbler, less formed, but actual claims of suffering and of need in our surroundings? Does the cry in the tragic play muffle, even blot out, the cry in the street?[30]

Part of the answer, as far as tragedy in particular is concerned, involves the desirability of developing and fostering certain 'structures of feeling'. Discussing the problem of television violence, Northrop Frye wrote that, 'In all scenes of violence there is the choice of identifying either with the agent or with the victim of violence. . . . The path of genuine education has to go through identification with the victim.'[31] The focused intensity of tragic art assists and accelerates those constant modifications of thought by feeling and feeling by thought which Wordsworth spoke of as helping to form our sensibility. In forcing us to share in the tormented conscience of a spy and murderer, or the anguish of an incestuous brother and sister, Webster and Ford push back the boundaries of human sympathy, making demands on us which go far beyond the 'easy' tears derided by Peter Brook. The inevitable selectivity and focusing involved in any immediate appeal to our feelings, whatever extension of sympathy may be involved, is probably a necessary concession to our inability to withstand psychologically the demands made upon us by all of the millions of others with whom we are figuratively, if not literally, in a 'face to face' relationship. Primo Levi wrote that,

> There is no proportion between the pity we feel and the extent of the pain by which the pity is aroused: a single Anne Frank excites more emotion than the myriads who suffered as she did but whose image has remained in the shadows. Perhaps it is necessary that it can be so; if we had to and were able to suffer the sufferings of everyone, we could not live. Perhaps the dreadful gift of pity for the many is granted only to saints . . . to all of us there remains in the best of cases, only the sporadic pity addressed to the single individual, the *Mitmensch*, the co-man: the human being of flesh and blood standing before us, within the reach of our providentially myopic senses.[32]

2
Webster and Jacobean Theatre

John Webster's known involvement with the theatre happens to be almost exactly coterminous with the reign of James I (1603–25). We first hear of him in May 1602 as one of five dramatists paid by Henslowe for their work on a lost tragedy called *Caesar's Fall* (or *Two Shapes*). The last definitely datable play in which he had a hand was *The Fair Maid of the Inn* (licensed for performance in 1626), though this may have been followed by his Roman tragedy *Appius and Virginia*. For the general reader or theatre-goer, with knowledge only of *The White Devil* or *The Duchess of Malfi*, Webster is probably *the* typical Jacobean dramatist, 'Jacobean' signifying a theatrically sophisticated and self-conscious preoccupation with extreme situations and motivations, accompanied by a melancholic and satiric brooding upon death, sexuality and court corruption. In fact, only a small proportion of Jacobean plays could be so characterised, but, taking into account the whole body of Webster's work, he could be seen as typically Jacobean in a much broader sense. To map his career is to come close to mapping Jacobean theatre itself.

Webster collaborated on plays with Dekker, Heywood, Middleton, Rowley, Fletcher, Massinger and Ford. He was strongly influenced by Marston, Chapman, Jonson and Shakespeare (as well as the Elizabethans Marlowe and Kyd). He wrote plays for both children's and adult companies, for both indoor ('private')

16

and outdoor ('public') theatres. He tried his hand at popular history (*Sir Thomas Wyatt*), city comedy (the *Ho* plays), Shakespearean tragedy (*The Duchess of Malfi*), dramatised journalism (*A Late Murder of the Son upon the Mother*), civic pageantry (the Lord Mayor's show of 1624), and Fletcherian tragicomedy (*A Cure for a Cuckold*). This kind of versatility – moving easily between different companies, theatres and genres, sometimes working in collaboration and sometimes alone – was typical of the period. Middleton's career presents a very similar picture. What is slightly odd about Webster is that his reputation derives from only two of his plays, performed within a couple of years of each other. He begins as an anonymous worker on the Elizabethan production line and ends in similar fashion, but in between manages to write two highly distinctive masterpieces.

Such a career challenges any absolute distinction between the austere literary genius of Romantic and Modernist mythology – a Flaubert or a Joyce devoted to their art rather than their public – and the unambitious hack working to a commercially successful formula. Webster did what was necessary to earn his living from the theatre but he was also an intensely self-conscious and ambitious artist who seized his opportunity to 'leave something so written to aftertimes, as they should not willingly let it die'.[1] The consistently high level of Shakespeare's output through twenty-three years and thirty-seven plays causes us to forget that wherever writing takes place in a highly pressured commercial environment it is common to find wild fluctuations of achievement. Modern science fiction could furnish many examples of writers capable equally of complex, challenging work and empty, hastily written formula pieces. What is perhaps rather unusual about early seventeenth-century theatre is that, through the constant critical input of men like Jonson and Chapman and the theoretically mute but practically persuasive example of Shakespeare, the peer-group pressure on aspiring writers was as much aesthetic as commercial. Webster wanted to sell his plays to companies of actors in a highly competitive marketplace, but he also, at least some of the time, wanted to write literature that would be remembered. For instance, when *The Duchess of Malfi* was printed in 1623, Webster referred to it as a 'poem' or 'work', terms which connoted a more prestigious literary achievement than 'play'. These literary ambitions meant that, like Jonson, Webster could be arrogant and insecure in his relationship with audiences, but he also shared with Jonson a deep awareness of popular taste and a capacity to satisfy it when he chose. This mixture of self-conscious sophistication with strong popular appeal is characteristic of major Jacobean plays.

The implied distinction between 'Elizabethan' and 'Jacobean' which is operative in this chapter is not wholly arbitrary but it is chronologically inexact and overemphasises the importance of the change of monarch. Many of the distinctive features of Jacobean drama derive from developments in the last few years of Elizabeth's reign. It was under Elizabeth that Jonson wrote his first comedies and under Elizabeth that Shakespeare embarked on his sequence of tragedies. In fact, if one is looking for the date which inaugurated a new phase in the history of the theatre, then 1599 seems more significant than 1603. During the second half of the 1590s the London theatre had been dominated by two companies of adult players, the Chamberlain's Men (for whom Shakespeare worked) and the Admiral's Men (who possessed Marlowe's plays). Both companies played at large open-air theatres and aimed at a broadly based audience in which the middle-class 'citizen' stratum of society was probably the dominant element.

In 1599, however, these companies were challenged by the re-emergence of a group of child actors playing at the tiny indoor theatre attached to St Paul's church. This theatre seated only 200 (compared with the 3000 who could be fitted into the outdoor theatres) and its higher admission charges created a more exclusive audience, composed mainly of gentry, courtiers, lawyers and Inns of Court students. The first plays written for this new venue, those of John Marston, are quite unlike anything in the pre-existing adult repertory in the way they sacrifice story and character in favour of stylistic excesses and sophisticated metatheatrical and parodic effects. The success of these plays soon led to another children's company, the Chapel Boys, beginning performances at the Blackfriars theatre, but the most important consequence was the effect on the adult companies. What emerges in the early years of the seventeenth century is not a simple opposition between two 'rival traditions' but a complicated pattern of cross-influence which shapes the art of all the major dramatists. 'Jacobean' drama really begins in 1599 and

Webster is the heir of both Shakespeare and Marston. How one reads his plays depends very much on which influence one chooses to emphasise.

Webster was born in London about 1578, coming from a similar social background to that of Marlowe and Shakespeare – comfortably middle-class rather than gentry. His father was a prosperous coachmaker living in the parish of St Sepulchre-without-Newgate, near Smithfield. He was a member of the Merchant Taylors Company, there being as yet no separate company for coachmakers. The family business (which was carried on by Webster's brother) is glanced at in a poem of 1617 which talks of 'crabbed Websterio, / The playwright-cartwright',[2] a phrase which seems to combine an aesthetic and social gibe in suggesting that Webster is an artisan rather than an artist. Webster's father was involved in every aspect of the transport business, which included the hiring out of wagons for plays and pageants and providing hearses for funerals. There are records of transactions with the actor Edward Alleyn and the dramatist Dekker.

However, the most interesting document relating to John Webster senior has only an oblique connection with the coach trade. In 1605 another Merchant Taylor, Robert Dove, endowed £50 to St Sepulchre's parish with the intention of providing spiritual help for condemned men at the nearby Newgate prison. The night before their execution they were to be visited by someone appointed by the parish who would ring a handbell and urge them to repent of their sins. Similar exhortations, accompanied by further bellringing, would be offered the following morning when the cart taking them to the gallows at Tyburn stopped outside St Sepulchre's church. The purpose of these efforts was to put prisoners 'in minde of their mortalitie' so as 'to awake their sleepie senses from securitie, to save their soules from perishing'.[3] Webster's father was one of twenty-four signatories to this bequest, no doubt signing as a leading and God-fearing member of his parish but also, perhaps, with a personal connection as the provider of execution carts. Here we obviously have the source for one of the roles that Bosola takes upon himself in Act IV of *The Duchess of Malfi*:

I am the common bellman,
That usually is sent to condemn'd persons
The night before they suffer.

(IV. ii. 173–5)

The original context makes abundantly clear that Bosola's claim
to be the Duchess's comforter ('Come, be of comfort, I will save
your life') is meant to be more than an ironic piece of gallows
humour. Webster made a further use of this motif in *The Devil's
Law-Case* when, following the duel between Contarino and
Ercole, a friar enters with 'two bellmen' to urge prayers for the
two supposedly dead nobles (II. iii. 78).

The young Webster was probably educated at the famous
Merchant Taylors' grammar school and he may have gone on to
study law at the Inns of Court. A 'John Webster' was admitted
to the Middle Temple (one of the four Inns) in 1598 and this may
well have been the dramatist. The Inns functioned very much as
England's 'third University' and the young men who hung
around London whilst trying to pick up a smattering of legal
training formed an important section of the theatre audiences.
They also provided from their ranks a number of the playwrights
(both Marston and Ford were for a time members of the Middle
Temple). The abundance of legal references and trial scenes in
Webster's plays has sometimes been cited in support of his having been an Inns of Court student but these things are equally
well explained by reference to the prevailing culture. It was a
highly litigious age and, moreover, legal questions are often a
way of bringing into focus larger social and political issues.
Much of the opposition to the Stuarts was fomented by lawyers
and took a legalistic form. The frequency of trial scenes in
Jacobean drama, like the widespread use of revenge plots, points
to a pervasive concern with justice which is not limited to those
dramatists with a legal background.

In the earliest records of Webster's involvement with the professional theatre, he appears as one of a team of collaborators
supplying plays at great speed for the adult companies. *Caesar's
Fall, Lady Jane* and *Christmas Comes But Once a Year* all belong to
this period, but the only text that has survived is *The Famous History of Sir Thomas Wyatt*, which is probably a condensed version
of the two parts of *Lady Jane* (1602). It was written for Worcester's

Men, a third adult troupe which had begun playing in London shortly before the death of Elizabeth, and the title page of the quarto credits it to Dekker and Webster (though they were probably not the only writers involved). It deals with the turbulent events following the death of Edward VI and accession of Mary, including the brief reign and subsequent trial and execution of Lady Jane Grey. As a piece of popular theatre, it was doubtless designed to cash in on the widespread fears of a succession crisis as Elizabeth approached her end but, like many Elizabethan history plays, it seems a scrappy piece of work, cramming in more episodes than it is capable of developing satisfactorily.

However, it is full of interesting anticipations of Webster's later work. The struggle for power at court leads to dizzying reversals of fortune, Machiavellian betrayals, principled but disastrous changes of allegiance, and the deaths of innocents. Installed as Queen in the Tower of London, Jane, like the Duchess of Malfi, sees her palace become her prison. Northumberland is arrested for treason by the same men who authorised his actions against Mary. Wyatt, like Bosola, changes sides at a crucial point in the play but to no avail. Jane and her husband Guildford Dudley are tried and condemned by judges who once supported their cause ('Who cride so loude as you, God save Queene *Iane*?'). There are occasional bitter outbursts which have the satirical force of the later Webster ('Great men like great Flies, through lawes Cobwebs breake') but most of the ironies are situational rather than elaborated into a railing commentary. The emotional centre of the play is to be found not in satiric anger but in the pathos of Jane's fall and death, something which needs to be borne in mind when discussing *The Duchess of Malfi*. As in the later play, there is a fascination with the way a member of the 'weaker' sex can face death with both courage and Christian humility. Her husband tells her:

I am a man, men better brooke the shocke
Of threatning death, your sexe are ever weake.
The thoughts of death, a womans hearte will breake.

(V. ii. 98–100)

But it is he who faints, she who is better 'armde to die'. The direct appeal to emotion at the end of *Sir Thomas Wyatt*, as an

innocent young woman confronts her executioner, is characteristic of 'popular' art rather than the more cynical and
self-conscious theatre of Marston. Later representations of the
same scene, such as Paul Delaroche's nineteenth-century painting of *The Execution of Lady Jane Grey*, have a similarly direct
emotional impact which ensures their continued popularity. As
far as Webster is concerned, the important thing is to remember
that his theatrical apprenticeship involved learning how to satisfy citizen tastes as well as private-theatre audiences.

His next surviving plays, *Westward Ho* (1604) and *Northward
Ho* (1605), are also collaborations with Dekker but written for the
Paul's Boys. City comedies based on sexual intrigue, they are
more genial and less pointedly satirical than similar plays by
Marston and Middleton, but nevertheless seem to have appealed
to the select audience at the tiny Paul's theatre. Plays with a realistic London setting were still something of a novelty and the
success of *Westward Ho* prompted Marston, Chapman and Jonson
to write the better-known *Eastward Ho* for the rival boys' company at the Blackfriars, helping to create a sub-genre which
flourished for the next few years, yielding plays like *The Alche-
mist* and *A Chaste Maid in Cheapside*.

For obvious generic reasons, there is little to connect the *Ho*
plays with Webster's mature tragedies but, about the same time
that he was writing *Westward Ho*, he was engaged on a smaller
but more significant assignment. Marston had written a satirical
tragicomedy, *The Malcontent*, for the Blackfriars Boys, but subsequently the manuscript had fallen into the hands of the King's
Men (as Shakespeare's company were now called). Ignoring any
possible breach of business ethics, they proceeded to perform the
play, with certain 'additions' provided by Marston himself and
Webster. The most substantial of these additions is a clever
Induction (probably the work of Webster) in which the actors Sly,
Sinklo, Burbage, Condell and Lowin discuss the play which is to
follow, Sly and Sinklo posing as members of the audience, the
rest 'playing themselves'. Marston had used a similar framing
device for *Antonio and Mellida*, and it has been argued that the
effect is to discourage identification with the characters and
manoeuvre the audience into taking a much more detached and
critical attitude to the action that is about to unfold. Such an
interpretation is most plausible when applied to the children's

companies with their more limited and stylised forms of acting. But one can also argue that the collapse of conventional distinctions between character, actor and spectator can be a source of emotional and psychological disturbance rather than a spur to intellectual analysis, especially when such effects are channelled through the more powerfully mimetic performances of an actor like Burbage. Both Shakespeare and Webster were influenced by Marston, but the metatheatrical devices in tragedies written for adult companies are not necessarily Marstonian in effect.

This is an important point which will be returned to in later chapters. What is indisputable is the significance of *The Malcontent* as a literal example of the crossovers between different theatrical styles in the early seventeenth century. The successful transfer from the Chapel Boys to the King's Men of this satiric Italianate tragicomedy (itself strongly influenced by *Hamlet*) helped to shape the whole course of Jacobean tragedy. Vindice, Flamineo and Bosola are all sons of Malevole, the 'spitting critic' of court corruption. If *Sir Thomas Wyatt* best represents the 'popular' strand in Webster, then his work on *The Malcontent* is the best example of his early exposure to a radically different kind of theatre.

Between 1605 and 1612, the year of *The White Devil*, there is a mysterious gap in Webster's career, with no evidence of any dramatic activity.[4] So many Jacobean plays have been lost without trace that we cannot infer anything very much from this absence of evidence but it is nevertheless suggestive of a prolonged brooding and painstaking effort, which was to result in work of markedly superior quality. In his address 'To the Reader' which prefaces *The White Devil*, Webster himself refers to the long period of gestation which preceded his first major work: 'To those who report I was a long time in finishing this tragedy, I confess I do not write with a goose-quill, winged with two feathers.' He justifies himself by suggesting that his work, like that of Euripides, will continue to be read for 'three ages' rather than the 'three days' which is the lifespan of more hastily written plays. Given the years of labour that Webster put into *The White Devil*, it must have been bitterly disappointing when it failed to please its first audience, as Webster's Preface makes clear. Like Ben Jonson and Oscar Wilde on similar occasions, the piqued playwright took the line that the play was a great success, it was the audience which was the failure. Subsequent critics have tended to follow Webster in seeing the play, performed by Queen Anne's Men at the Red Bull, as ill-suited to its particular venue, so a brief account of the theatrical situation in 1612 is desirable at this point.

Following the accession of James, the three main adult companies had all acquired royal patrons, thus strengthening the existing links between drama and the court, links which were to prove fatal in 1642. Shakespeare's company, the Chamberlain's Men, had its leading status confirmed by becoming the King's Men, whilst the Admiral's and Worcester's companies became respectively Prince Henry's Men and Queen Anne's Men. It was the King's Men who had adapted most to the challenge posed by the various boys' companies, and in 1609 they themselves began playing at the indoor Blackfriars theatre in winter as well as the Globe in summer, thus appealing to two distinct but overlapping types of audience. The other two companies, playing at the Fortune and the Red Bull (open-air theatres in the northern suburbs), carried on with the same sort of popular repertoire rooted in spectacle and action which had pleased mass audiences in the 1590s. The Paul's Boys had ceased playing by 1607, their impact on English theatre out of all proportion to their brief history, and the other children's company was shortly to be merged with a fourth adult group, Lady Elizabeth's Men.

From its opening in 1605 until the closing of the theatres in 1642, the Red Bull was subject to numerous gibes about the unsophisticated nature of its audience and its repertoire. Even without hindsight, it looks as if Webster would have been better offering *The White Devil*, with its disconcerting mix of satirical commentary, densely poetic language and violent action, to the King's Men (who had successfully staged *The Revenger's Tragedy*). However, it is possible to read too much significance into a single afternoon's events. A combination of poor weather and a low turn-out ('it was acted, in so dull a time of winter, presented in so open and black a theatre, that it wanted . . . a full and understanding auditory') can destroy the impact of a play more thoroughly than some touches of over-sophistication. Despite its initial failure, *The White Devil* remained in the repertoire of the Queen's Men and continued to be played up until 1642, leaving behind a sufficient reputation to ensure its revival after the

Restoration. The play's fast-moving succession of violent and spectacular events was enough to guarantee its survival, despite the obvious difficulties it poses for any audience. The contrast with Jonson's *Sejanus* is instructive. Webster had the failure of this 'learned' tragedy in mind when he composed his own defensive Preface, but there is only tenuous evidence that Jonson's play was ever risked in the theatre again after its disastrous opening and it certainly never established itself firmly in the King's Men's repertoire.

The feeling that *The White Devil* is a reworking and recombination of most of the important styles of early Jacobean theatre is confirmed by the Preface, which lists Chapman, Jonson, Beaumont, Fletcher, Shakespeare, Dekker and Heywood as fellow dramatists whom Webster admires to the extent of wishing that what he writes 'may be read by their light'. The list spans the range of theatrical possibilities from the self-consciously weighty political tragedies of Chapman and Jonson, to the unashamedly popular spectacles provided by Heywood (the principal dramatist of the Queen's Men). The only significant omission is Marston, which may reflect an 'anxiety of influence' on Webster's part or simply a concern not to embarrass Marston, who by this time had abandoned the theatre to become a clergyman and might not appreciate allusions to his earlier career. If from one point of view Webster's major works seem like echo-chambers of previous plays, thus confirming post-structuralist scepticism about 'the author' as a point of creative origin, from another standpoint it needs to be emphasised that, out of the mass of theatrical formulae and 'discourses' available, he succeeded briefly in creating his own 'voice'. In the absence of any information about the authorship of *The White Devil* and *The Duchess of Malfi* there is no other playwright to whom they could confidently be attributed, however many specific borrowings and echoes can be detected.

The White Devil was published within a year of its first performance, an unusually rapid passage into print which probably means that the company did not regard the script as a particularly 'hot' property which needed to be safeguarded from the eyes of rivals and, secondly, that Webster was anxious to prove to the world that, contrary to the ill-informed opinion of the Red Bull audience, he *had* succeeded in producing a masterpiece.

Someone connected with the King's Men must have been impressed because London's leading company were happy to commission from Webster *The Duchess of Malfi*, which opened at the Blackfriars theatre probably in the winter of 1613–14. At the Blackfriars Webster found his 'understanding auditory' and achieved his greatest success. Many scenes in the play seem designed to take advantage of the increased intimacy and artificial lighting found at the indoor theatre, finding their emotional focus in moments of stillness rather than violent action or spectacle, and Webster's complex plotting would not have confused spectators used to the plays of Fletcher, who had replaced Shakespeare as the company's leading dramatist. Moreover, in creating a central character with whom audiences can emotionally identify, Webster was making his play more Shakespearean, moving closer to the strengths of popular theatre without sacrificing the satirical edge he learnt from Marston. Several tributes from fellow dramatists were attached to the printed edition of the play and both Middleton and Rowley seem to locate the heart of the play's appeal in the figure of the Duchess, something which is borne out in most modern productions but not always registered in modern criticism. The most eloquent tribute, however, came from John Ford, who was not afraid to rank Webster with the revered tragic writers of antiquity:

> Crown him a poet, whom nor Rome, nor Greece,
> Transcend in all theirs, for a masterpiece.

The Duchess of Malfi continued to be played by the King's Men up until the closing of the theatres, its selection as one of the plays to be put on at court in 1630 giving clear testimony to its continued popularity. In writing for the leading company of actors one of their most successful plays, John Webster had reached the high-point of his career.

A lost play, which Webster refers to as *Guise*, may have followed *The Duchess of Malfi* but the next, and last, of his unaided compositions to survive is the tragicomedy *The Devil's Law-Case*, which was first performed between about 1617 and 1619. To consider this play is to bring into focus two of the most important theatrical developments of the second half of James's reign. The first of these is the increasingly dominant influence of John

Fletcher, Shakespeare's successor. Building on characters and situations which Shakespeare had made popular, Fletcher (with his collaborators) provided plays of every genre for the King's Men, but brought to particular perfection a species of tragicomedy which relied on complicated twists of plot to bring potentially disastrous events to a happy ending. In imitating Marston, Webster had already, in his earlier work, exploited a form of tragicomedy in which violence and horror are mingled with satirical laughter, but *The Devil's Law-Case* is his first play to be plotted in the manner of Fletcher. It also may have been one of the first plays to be written for an important new indoor theatre, the Cockpit (or Phoenix) in Drury Lane.

This had been built in 1616 by Christopher Beeston (who managed the Queen's Men) in a bid to imitate the success the King's Men had achieved playing at the indoor Blackfriars as well as the outdoor Globe. However, rather than leave his players at the Red Bull during the summer months, he transferred them and their entire repertoire to the Cockpit on a permanent basis. There is an important point worth making about this. Despite all those histories of the theatre which emphasise the fissure between the tastes of 'private' and 'public' theatre audiences in the years following Shakespeare's retirement, the fact that Beeston could successfully transfer actors and plays from the roughest of the northern amphitheatres to what became an immediately fashionable indoor theatre near to the Inns of Court suggests that the differences between venues were more social than aesthetic. When a mob of apprentices wrecked the Cockpit on Shrove Tuesday in 1617, they were not making a general criticism of alien theatrical tastes but registering anger that their own favourite plays had been removed from their local theatre and put beyond their price range. Beeston quickly repaired the Cockpit and continued to move companies and plays between it and the Red Bull for the rest of James's reign. *The Devil's Law-Case* looks as if it was designed to please a Cockpit audience, but it may well have been performed from time to time at the Red Bull, given the complicated interchanges between the two theatres.

For the remainder of his career, Webster reverted to a pattern of undistinguished collaboration with a number of different dramatists working for different companies. *Anything for a Quiet Life* (c.1621), a city comedy written with Middleton for the King's

Men, transposes the topic of powerful and wayward women from Italian courts to the streets of London. The lost *A Late Murder of the Son upon the Mother* (1624), written with Ford, Dekker and Rowley for the Red Bull theatre, was an attempt to cash in quickly on sensational local events and, if it had survived, would have given us a striking example of Webster and Ford as tabloid journalists to set against the more familiar, and equally valid, picture of them as self-conscious tragic artists. Our knowledge of the play is, in fact, derived mainly from the libel suits it provoked.

A Cure for a Cuckold (*c*.1625), a Fletcherian tragicomedy written with Rowley for an unknown company, is interesting because it presents in extreme form some of the problems of characterisation and motivation which have preoccupied critics of the major plays. It is an exasperating play to read (at one point Webster's editor, F. L. Lucas, felt driven to emend the text simply to impose some consistency on the character of Clare) but where it seems least satisfactory, as in IV. ii (generally agreed to be written by Webster), is also where it seems closest to greatness. One can condemn the bewildering twists and turns of the characters in this scene as the product of a slack attempt to imitate Fletcher's style of plotting but nevertheless be impressed by Webster's continuing capacity to convey a brittle emotional instability, producing violently obsessional behaviour and surges of contradictory feelings in characters whose 'true' motives are opaque even to themselves. This kind of capacity is a much rarer dramatic gift than the ability to maintain a simple consistency of motivation.

All that now remained before Webster's death in the 1630s was a share in another tragicomedy, *The Fair Maid of the Inn* (1626) written with Fletcher, Ford and Massinger for the King's Men, and a collaboration with Heywood on a Roman tragedy, *Appius and Virginia* (of uncertain date and provenance). None of Webster's later work has attracted much modern critical attention and none of it provoked the enthusiasm of contemporaries in the way that *The Duchess of Malfi* evidently did. Nevertheless it is clear he remained trusted as a competent craftsman who would fulfil whatever task he was given by a company to the best of his ability. There is little sign of the high literary ambitions voiced in the Preface to *The White Devil*, but perhaps he felt he had done enough to achieve his immortality. In writing *Appius and Virginia* with Heywood he was bringing his career full-circle since his first dramatic collaboration had been on another Roman tragedy, the lost *Caesar's Fall*. In fact, *Appius and Virginia* reads like a play from an earlier period since its straightforward construction and characterisation bear no signs of the influence of Fletcher (or Marston either, for that matter). The appearance of Shakespeare's Roman plays in the First Folio of 1623 may have been the spur to this apparently old-fashioned project. Despite all the developments and shifts of taste charted by theatre historians, one needs to remember that through constant revivals and reprintings all the different phases of the drama enjoyed a synchronous co-existence. All possible forms and styles were simultaneously available, a state of affairs that would be called post-modernist if it occurred in the 1990s. In the course of his career, Webster exploited most of these forms and styles but only for a brief period was he able to construct his own dramatic 'voice' from them.

This chapter has so far concentrated on the theatrical context but the nature of Webster's major plays makes it equally important to say something about their political and religious background.[5] Chapman's *Bussy D'Ambois* (1604), a tragedy which Webster undoubtedly admired, begins with the protagonist complaining bitterly that 'Fortune, not Reason, rules the state of things' and there seems to be a deliberate ambiguity about the last phrase, leaving one uncertain whether Bussy is voicing a metaphysical complaint about the universe or a political complaint about the state. The same ambiguity recurs at the end of the play when the dying hero cries despairingly, 'let my death / Define life nothing but a Courtier's breath' (V. iii. 131–2). The tendency of Marxist-influenced criticism has been to analyse the metaphysical questionings in Jacobean tragedy as a projection of social and political anxieties rooted in a specific historical context. However, the word 'specific' (somewhat overworked in modern criticism) can easily have a mesmeric effect, producing a misleading emphasis on the distinction between 'Jacobean' and 'Elizabethan' and ascribing too much to special characteristics of the Jacobean court.

In general terms, the Renaissance had seen a concentration of political power at the centre. In England, the regional power of provincial barons and the supranational power of the Catholic church had both been broken by the Tudors. The court had become the perceived centre of national life and culture, so that if the court was corrupt then the entire nation was seen to be infected. Nowhere is this better expressed than in the famous lines at the beginning of *The Duchess of Malfi*, whose admonitory force is sharpened by the potentially subversive collocation of 'court' and 'common' (a word frequently used negatively in such phrases as 'common sewer' or 'common whore' as well as positively, as in 'common weal'):

> a Prince's court
> Is like a common fountain, whence should flow
> Pure silver-drops in general. But if't chance
> Some curs'd example poison't near the head,
> *Death and diseases through the whole land spread.*
>   (I. i. 11–15)

The savage attacks on court life in Webster's plays and many other early seventeenth-century tragedies seem to register a deep and widespread conviction that something was rotten at the heart of the state. Many of the known abuses of the Jacobean court – conspicuous consumption, sycophancy, bribery, the exploitation of monopoly rights – were given extensive dramatic treatment, and many characters, like Webster's Vittoria, died with imprecations against the court on their lips:

> O happy they that never saw the court,
> Nor ever knew great man but by report.
>   (V. vi. 259–60)

However, any attempt to relate the political thrust of the drama directly to actual political developments quickly runs into a number of complications. Jacobean tragedies do not simply record, as part of a process leading to civil war, a growing lack of confidence in the Stuart monarchy. During the early years of his reign James enjoyed a good deal of popularity as fears of chaos following the death of Elizabeth proved unfounded and the ex-

pensive, seemingly endless war with Spain was concluded with
a peace treaty. The Gunpowder Plot of 1605, like modern IRA
bombs, did more to strengthen national solidarity than undermine it. All the major scandals and disasters of James's rule – the
Overbury trials of 1615–16, the Cockayne disaster during the
same years, the fall of Lord Treasurer Suffolk in 1618, the foreign
policy crisis which began with the Thirty Years' War – came in
the latter half of the reign. A number of late Jacobean plays do
attack specific royal policies, notably James's refusal to commit
himself to the Protestant cause in the Thirty Years' War, but a
glance at the dates of various plays is enough to show that the
most intense attacks upon court life nearly all belong to the early
years of the century, the years of James's greatest popularity: *Sejanus* (1603), *The Malcontent* (1602–4), *Bussy D'Ambois* (1604), *The
Revenger's Tragedy* (1606), *The White Devil* (1612). Moreover, a
number of characteristically 'Jacobean' political tragedies are in
fact Elizabethan, notably *Antonio's Revenge* and *Hamlet* (both
c.1600), and an Elizabethan dating for both *Sejanus* and *The Malcontent* is quite probable. Shakespeare's most famous tragedy
enacts with particular power the image of an ulcer at the heart
of the court spreading its poison through the entire body politic.

Since these late Elizabethan plays were particularly influential
on Jacobean tragedy, one obvious possible conclusion is that the
drama may exist in a real but perpetually displaced relation to
social and political events. Plays written in the context of a dis-
illusion with the last years of Elizabeth's reign – years of war,
inflation, bitter factionalism at court, and increasingly erratic and
autocratic behaviour by the ageing Queen – were artistically
powerful enough to generate their own theatrical momentum,
provoking a succession of imitations lasting for several years into
James's reign.[6] Such an argument acknowledges that the primary
influence on literature is always previous literature, without trying to seal off drama altogether from society. More simply,
bearing in mind that *Hamlet* and *Antonio's Revenge* were themselves imitating earlier Elizabethan plays concerned with justice
and power, and that these earlier plays drew upon Senecan mod-
els, one could argue that many of the grievances against the
workings of the court remain broadly similar whether one is
talking about Nero, Lodovico Sforza, Elizabeth or James.
Ralegh's great and bitter poem 'The Lie' ('Say to the Court it

glowes / and shines like rotten wood') was written in the 1590s, but it would have been an equally appropriate expression of his feelings in 1608, when it was first published. The Roman or six-teenth-century Italian settings of Jacobean court tragedies were perceived as relevant to the seventeenth-century political context because, as Fulke Greville wrote, 'the vices of former ages being so like to these of this age as it will be easy to find out some affinity or resemblance between them'.[7] It is partly because these plays' relentless concern with power and subjection is *not* narrowly specific that they can continue to engage audiences unfamiliar with the Jacobean context but with more recent experiences of the unjust and corrupt workings of authority to draw upon.

No brief account of the political context would be complete without drawing attention to the basic paradox that, despite providing the most eloquent criticism of the court's abuses, the drama remained dependent on the court for protection and patronage. Although they were self-supporting commercial enterprises, the theatre companies would not have been able to survive the civic and Puritan opposition they aroused without the backing of the court, as was demonstrated by the closing of the theatres in 1642 after the king had lost control of London. The court was able to satisfy its need for regular, high-quality enter-tainment by ensuring that professional theatre continued to flourish in the capital. The mutual advantages of this arrange-ment may help to explain why, as the Stuarts' political problems increased, the theatre was prepared to attack particular royal policies but not to continue dramatising a wholesale and irreme-diable corruption at the centre.

Tragedy, by virtue of its concern with suffering and evil, almost inevitably raises religious and philosophical questions, and the ways in which these are articulated obviously vary his-torically. Webster's plays, like other tragedies of the period, are deeply marked by the religious anxieties which attended the Ref-ormation. The great schism within Christianity set families, communities and nations against one another in bloody wars of religion. Smithfield, adjoining Webster's parish of St Sepulchre's, had been the site of the Protestant martyrdoms under Mary, and Webster himself may have witnessed there the burning of an Arian heretic in 1612. No wonder Flamineo says bitterly that 'The first bloodshed in the world happened about religion' (*The*

White Devil, V. iii. 39–40). As well as promoting civil strife, the Protestant challenge to Catholicism helped to relativise the whole notion of religious 'truth'. Vicious theological disputations foregrounded some of the most awkward and contentious aspects of Christian belief and what was deemed 'true' varied according to which monarch was on the throne. The Third Madman in *The Duchess of Malfi* cries despairingly, 'Greek is turn'd Turk; we are only to be saved by the Helvetian translation' (IV. ii. 91–2). The broad medieval path to salvation has here narrowed to an anxious sectarian reliance on one particular translation of the Bible, the Genevan version with its Calvinist commentaries.

To understand the literature of the early seventeenth century it is crucial to realise that the theological orthodoxy prevailing in England was strongly Calvinist.[8] The Elizabethan 'compromise' between Catholicism and Protestantism had been a compromise over forms of worship and church organisation rather than matters of doctrine. The grim Calvinist insistence that the majority of people were predestined to damnation with no possibility of redeeming themselves remained part of Anglican orthodoxy until the Arminian counter-movement of the 1620s. The Thirty-nine Articles of 1571 had incorporated references to predestined salvation but had chosen not to emphasise the depressing corollary. The Lambeth Articles of 1595, authorised by Archbishop Whitgift, had no such inhibitions:

I: God from eternity has predestined some men to life, and reprobated some to death. . . .

IV: Those not predestined to salvation are inevitably condemned on account of their sins. . . .

IX: It is not in the will or the power of each and every man to be saved.[9]

Only the personal opposition of Elizabeth herself prevented these unequivocal declarations being publicly promulgated as required doctrines of the English Church. The Calvinist God believed in by most Anglican divines was an inscrutable deity whose prior decisions about who were to be saved and who damned were inaccessible to human reason and hence a source of perpetual spiritual anxiety. Such a terrible theology did not command universal assent in the Shakespeare period. Important bishops like Lancelot Andrewes did not subscribe to it and the degree to which 'ordinary' churchgoers, especially in rural areas, were in thrall to it remains a matter of continuing dispute. However, it remained the dominant orthodoxy, subscribed to by 'moderate' Anglican clergy as well as Puritans, until challenged by Laud in the reign of Charles I, a challenge which helped to provoke the civil war.

The impression one gets from Webster's plays that many of his characters are caught in traps which are not of their own choosing has a theological as well as a political context. The most striking example of this is Bosola, whose every impulse to do good is mysteriously and cruelly frustrated, leaving him at the end of the play as a 'wretched thing of blood'. The inexorable Fate against which Webster's characters cry out ('Fate's a spaniel, / We cannot beat it from us') often seems to be a displacement into classical terms of distinctively Calvinist anxieties. However, any Calvinist reading of Webster's plays is complicated by the presence of pre-Reformation redemptive patterns and by the ambiguities of their Italian Catholic settings. Theologically, as in all other respects, the major plays remain enigmatic, capable of sponsoring a variety of interpretations.

3
The White Devil

In Act I of *The White Devil*, Vittoria's adulterous meeting with Duke Brachiano, aided and attended by her Moorish servant Zanche and pandar-brother Flamineo, is violently interrupted by her mother Cornelia who bursts from her hiding-place to utter a moral denunciation. Flamineo responds angrily with 'What Fury rais'd thee up? away, away!' (I. ii. 268) but, puzzlingly, it is Zanche rather than Cornelia who exits. In Act V, with Vittoria and Brachiano now married following the murder of their previous spouses, Flamineo is enjoying some dalliance of his own with Zanche when Cornelia bursts in again, this time to insult and strike the black woman before rushing away again immediately.

A consideration of these two brief episodes brings out a number of important points about Webster's dramaturgy. There is an apparent recourse to traditional theatrical symbolism (black faces on the Elizabethan and Jacobean stage were always potentially sinister through their association with the black-faced devils of medieval drama) but this symbolism is exploited in an ambiguous and riddling manner. As she spreads out a carpet and cushions for the adulterous lovers, Zanche's appearance may indeed carry diabolic connotations and her immediate exit following the 'virtuous' Cornelia's outburst carries hints of a successful exorcism. However, the way Cornelia is addressed by

Flamineo ('What Fury rais'd thee up?') associates her too with the powers of hell and there is a disturbingly violent edge to her righteousness. When she kneels to curse Vittoria – 'If thou dishonour thus thy husband's bed, / Be thy life short as are the funeral tears / In great men's' (I. ii. 292–4) – there is a prefiguration of the murderous 'friars' who kneel at Brachiano's bedside cursing him in his last moments and telling him that he will be forgotten before his funeral sermon. In the second encounter with Zanche, which is obviously meant to recall the first, the violence of Cornelia's anger turns to actual blows and the context makes it even more difficult to see this as a straightforward expression of 'the strong antipathy of good to bad'. Cornelia has accompanied Brachiano and Vittoria to the Duke's court at Padua apparently without any qualms about the convenient deaths of Isabella and Camillo. Her attack on Zanche looks more like a piece of petty spite by someone who has abandoned the moral high ground but still craves the pleasures of self-righteousness.

It is clear from the above that Webster is presenting us with a world in which conventional distinctions between good and evil, white and black, are constantly invoked yet constantly undermined, a world in which characters are unstable and perpetually on the edge of violence, a world whose psychological and moral chaos is made fully apprehensible through devices of repetition, parallel and echo which bear witness to a high degree of artistic ordering. It is also clear that this is a play which will make heavy demands on its audience. Its moral ambiguities, its sudden shifts of perspective and changes of tone, its apparent discontinuities of characterisation all serve to challenge an audience in ways which often seem peculiarly 'modern'. In fact it is easier to describe some of Webster's techniques than it is to be sure about their overall effect. Some of the more plausible attempts to characterise this effect, such as linking Webster's dramaturgy to Brechtian theory, seem well wide of the mark when one actually experiences the play in the theatre.

Webster's habit of giving his own twist to conventional symbolism is immediately evident in the play's title. As used by his contemporaries, the phrase 'white devil' seems to signify moral hypocrisy of a relatively straightforward kind. This is how it is used by the preacher Thomas Adams in his sermon *The White*

Devil, or the Hypocrite Uncased, published the year after Webster's play and probably deliberately echoing its title. This is also how it is used in *The Revenger's Tragedy*, performed in 1606. When Vindice, in the process of murdering the Duke, denounces him as 'Royal villain, white devil', it is a moment of savage intensity – but the moral point is not in doubt. The Duke had seemed noble but was in actuality rotten to the core. By contrast, Webster seems to use the phrase in a more fully paradoxical way, suggesting the continuous interpenetration of good and evil in the human heart. It is even left uncertain to whom the title refers, stimulating the audience to attempt to apply it to a whole series of characters and in the process become involved in ever more complex moral evaluations.

The theatrical symbolism of black and white is used throughout to enforce this sense of moral paradox. Webster's model here is *Othello*, with its constant stage juxtaposition of noble black man and white villain, rather than the earlier and simpler *Titus Andronicus*, with its wholeheartedly devilish Moor, Aaron. As well as Zanche, who treacherously betrays her mistress before dying nobly alongside her, there are two other black faces in Webster's play. Francisco pursues his revenge by disguising himself as an Othello figure, a Christianised Moorish soldier, and there is a so-called 'ghost' character called 'little Jaques the Moor' who has no lines but who enters as a companion of young Giovanni at the beginning of Act II. J. R. Brown's Revels edition excises this figure from the stage direction, replacing him with anonymous 'Attendants', but he is surely an important part of Webster's overall conception, despite his silence. We have already seen Brachiano, Flamineo and Vittoria accompanied by Zanche, and in our first sight of the main opposed grouping of Francisco, Monticelso, Isabella, Marcello and Giovanni we also register the presence of a black face. Each of the major factions displays an enigmatic pattern of black and white, and the fact that the little prince Giovanni (who is to restore order at the end of the play) has a black shadow is particularly unsettling. The obvious importance of this kind of symbolism in the play has encouraged directors in recent years to cast black actors in several of the other roles. By making all of the Corombona family black, Philip Prowse (National Theatre, 1991) may have been trying to make the sociological point that Vittoria's family were members of a victimised underclass, but the Oxford Playhouse production of 1981 was probably closer to fulfilling Webster's riddling symbolism in its more random distribution of black actors throughout the play.

The use of Moorish characters is not the only way Webster develops this symbolism. The general visual irony of Brachiano's murderers arriving at his court dressed as crusaders is sharpened when we learn that they claim to belong to the order of St John of Jerusalem, whose official garb was a black robe decorated with a silver cross. We have already seen this striking costume on one of the ambassadors attending the election of the Pope, and the alternation of black and silver makes a neat moral and visual link between the murderers and the entire apparatus of church and state. A less clearcut effect occurs when Giovanni and Lodovico enter together to announce Isabella's death. It is disturbing to see the young prince in close company with the murderous and banished count and, since it is clear from the dialogue that Giovanni is dressed in the black of mourning, the troubling juxtaposition of the two figures would be highlighted if Lodovico were to wear white or black rather than anything intermediate.

These visual details, with their suggestions of moral ambiguity, find their full justification in Webster's conception of his characters. At times, in the manner of Marston, this veers towards a generalised satirical disgust – 'Is he not a courtly gentleman? (When he wears white satin one would take him by his black muzzle to be no other creature than a maggot)' (I. ii. 138–41) – but the deeper and more pervasive emphasis is on the extreme and unstable mixture of contrary impulses to be found in the human heart. The complexities of his characters become apparent not through a smooth pattern of development but through sudden glimpses of hitherto unsuspected qualities. Virtuous self-control gives way to sudden surges of violence, whilst apparently settled cynicism and brutality is briefly interrupted by compassion. The effect is frequently startling but it is not incoherent, though it requires actors capable of suggesting the 'inner life' which flows through the surface turbulence of their parts. For Emrys Jones, reviewing the 1991 National Theatre production, 'the power to convey the inward flow of consciousness is precisely what gives Webster his special quality' but he found this missing from the performance of Dhobi Oparei as Flamineo.[1] Like the rest of the cast, Oparei was struggling to impose himself on the huge Olivier stage, cluttered with a spectacular baroque (or 'Renaissance Gothic') set. Like all of Philip Prowse's numerous Webster productions, this was a marvellous example of designer's theatre but the Jacobean stage was essentially an actor's theatre and Webster himself wrote that 'the *Actor* is the *Center*'.[2] His plays need a style of production which allows actors to dominate their stage and their audience, projecting an emotional realism which feeds off the alleged inconsistencies in their parts. When good actors are left free to do this, 'we recognize in our surprise something even better than consistency – truth'.[3]

Catherine Belsey has argued that the peculiarly discontinuous presentation of Vittoria, the way she strikes different and unrelated attitudes in different scenes, is connected with the uncertain subject position occupied by women in the early seventeenth century.[4] However, there seems little reason to make a gender distinction since Webster's treatment of her is typical of his approach to nearly all the characters in the play. We see her from a number of different angles, a single line often being enough to effect a radical change of viewpoint, but there remains an irreducible uncertainty about her basic motivation. Given that she is often identified by critics as the white devil of the play, there is surprisingly little hard evidence of her actual guilt. Her involvement in the murders of Isabella and Camillo can only be inferred from the ambiguous dream which she recounts to Brachiano. As in actual dreams, the images are 'over-determined' (the yew-tree at one point seems to represent Camillo, at another Brachiano) and require the mediation of an interpreter, in this case Flamineo, who can hardly be described as reliable. In performance, the suggestion of criminal incitement comes across more strongly than on the printed page since the pun which identifies Brachiano with the lethal 'yew' is sounded more clearly, the narrative being interrupted at that precise point to increase the emphasis:

> VITTORIA: . . . there came stealing in
> Your Duchess and my husband; one of them
> A pick-axe bore, th'other a rusty spade,

And in rough terms they 'gan to challenge me,
About this yew.
BRACHIANO: That tree.
VITTORIA: This harmless yew.
                                              (I. ii. 235–9)

As she continues relating her dream, an air of intimate and col-
lusive menace develops, but no court could convict her on this
evidence, not even the hostile court she faces in Act III, and the
impression of her as a calculating murderess is in any case
severely qualified by the obvious distress she shows at her
mother's intervention – 'O me accurs'd' (I. ii. 299). These are the
last words she speaks before her trial, since she is offstage
throughout Act II, and their anguish jars strangely, though not
implausibly, with the self-assurance she projects in court. It is
easier to face a corrupt judge with courage than to laugh off the
curses of a mother.

In one of the scenes which Webster contributed to *The Fair
Maid of the Inn* there is a piece of stage business which superficially seems to recapitulate in miniature the general effect of the
trial scene in *The White Devil*. The mountebank Forobosco has
been exposed as a rogue but in response to his accusers he whirls
his cloak inside-out, turning it from the black of guilt to the
white of innocence:

I doe vilifie your censure – you demand if I am guilty, whir!
sayes my cloake by a tricke of legerdemaine, now I am not
guilty, I am guarded with innocence – pure silver lace I assure
you. (V. iii. 317–19)

Frank Dunlop may have had this incident in mind when he directed *The White Devil* for the National Theatre in 1969. In the
midst of her trial, Vittoria's white cloak fell away to reveal a
dress of flaming red, confirming her accusers' picture of her as a
'scarlet woman'. It is easy to see why the parallel with the
Forobosco incident might have made this seem a good idea, but
in fact it cheapens and coarsens Webster's presentation of Vittoria. Unlike Forobosco, she is not a self-evidently guilty figure
whose desperate stratagems to make the worse appear the better
cause are easily seen through by audience and characters alike.

Her performance in the trial is so perfect that, like Ford's Perkin Warbeck, it creates its own reality and leaves the audience with an unsolvable enigma to ponder rather than the satisfaction of penetrating a disguise. In her subsequent scenes she projects a range of emotions – tearful rage at Brachiano's unfounded jealousy, an intense wordless desire rekindled by his kiss, desolate grief at his death, meditative piety when Flamineo finds her at her prayers – whilst remaining elusive. It is typical of Webster not to seek to draw the various strands of her personality together in the fifth act. Indeed, her best and worst moments come in close succession at the end of the play. The animal savagery with which she and Zanche trample on Flamineo when they think they have outwitted him is followed immediately by the aristocratic poise with which she faces her own death.

Her lover, Duke Brachiano, presents almost as many faces to the audience. His opening exclamation, 'Quite lost Flamineo', encourages us to view him as a lovelorn Antony, prepared to kiss away kingdoms and provinces, but much of his behaviour suggests a cold, ruthless man whose desire for Vittoria is merely one aspect of an arrogant, aristocratic will which recognises no social or moral impediments to its fulfilment. At Vittoria's trial, he seems more concerned to safeguard his own position than to defend his mistress, despite having earlier boasted, 'I'll seat you above law and above scandal' (I. ii. 261). His thunderous words 'Nemo me impune lacessit' ['No one harms me with impunity'] are uttered as he stalks from the court, leaving Vittoria to face her accusers alone. His odd, brief re-entry immediately after her sentence, when he addresses Francisco in emollient terms ('Now you and I are friends sir'), does not suggest the behaviour of a devoted lover so much as renewed male solidarity once a bit of woman trouble has been sorted out. In Act IV, his violent and hypocritical abuse of Vittoria at the House of Convertites is also repellent but at least it seems to spring from some genuine passion, and later, in his death agonies, he sounds once more like an Antony: 'Where's this good woman? Had I infinite worlds / They were too little for thee' (V. iii. 18–19). Probably the most revealing glimpse of his character occurs when Flamineo, in one of those characteristic Websterian flashes of pride, rebels for once against his humiliating exploitation. Brachiano simply cannot conceive of any social inferior defying his will:

BRACHIANO: In you pander!
FLAMINEO: What me, my lord, am I your dog?
BRACHIANO: A blood-hound; do you brave? do you stand
   me?
FLAMINEO: Stand you? Let those that have diseases run;
   I need no plasters.
BRACHIANO: Would you be kick'd?
FLAMINEO: Would you have your neck broke?
   I tell you Duke, I am not in Russia;
   My shins must be kept whole.
   BRACHIANO: Do you know me?
                                        (IV. ii. 49–56)

Nowhere in the play is aristocratic insolence and hubris better
articulated, and Webster makes us fully aware of the petty spite-
fulness of 'great men' when he later shows Brachiano taking
revenge upon Flamineo for this momentary defiance.

Flamineo himself exists in a different relation to the audience
from either Vittoria or Brachiano since he acts as a commentator
on the play's events, frequently making use of asides and direct
address. In one way this brings him closer to us (literally closer,
since many of his asides need to be delivered from a downstage
position to be fully effective), but in being a medium of interpretation he is difficult to pin down as an object of interpretation. In
continually directing our gaze at others ('See, here he comes',
'See she comes'), he eludes scrutiny himself. He is pitched some-
where between the railing voices of earlier satirical plays ('Let
those that have diseases run' echoes one of Thersites' subversive
jokes) and more fully developed tragic figures like Bosola. His
extreme self-consciousness about the roles which life forces him
to play makes any claim to have grasped the 'real' Flamineo
seem naïve. Which better expresses the 'real' man, the brutal
murder of his brother (Marcello is stabbed from behind while ex-
amining the crucifix worn by their mother) or the stirrings of
compassion Flamineo feels at the subsequent funeral? In performance, it is the second moment that is usually more striking
because less expected and there have been many testimonies to
its emotional impact.[5] It hardly serves to 'fix' Flamineo for us as
a character but it emphasises the gap between Webster's art and
Marston's even when there is some superficial resemblance. We

never achieve the same degree of emotional intimacy with the satirical commentators in Marston's plays. Flamineo's mocking laughter carries with it an edge of existential anguish that is missing in the earlier dramatist:

> I have liv'd
> Riotously ill, like some that live in court.
> And sometimes, when my face was full of smiles
> Have felt the maze of conscience in my breast.
> Oft gay and honour'd robes those tortures try,
> *We think cag'd birds sing, when indeed they cry.*
>
> (V. iv. 117–22)

So many of the minor characters, despite the limited nature of their parts, behave in unexpected and contradictory ways that one is justified in assuming that a general principle of characterisation, taking its cue from the play's oxymoronic title, is in operation. The case of Cornelia has already been looked at and that of Marcello is very similar. Despite the virtuous speeches which establish his role as the 'good' brother, he too has accompanied Brachiano and Vittoria to Padua and he too relieves his feelings with a vicious physical assault on Zanche. His dying words may carry some hint of guilty self-knowledge as well as having a more obvious reference to Flamineo and Vittoria:

> There are some sins which heaven doth duly punish
> In a whole family. This it is to rise
> By all dishonest means.
>
> (V. ii. 20–2)

Likewise, Isabella, the wife of Brachiano, is primarily developed as a figure of innocent pathos. The brutality of Brachiano's refusal to kiss her, complaining of the foulness of her breath, and the painfully ironic corollary of her manner of death, kissing the poisoned picture of her husband, enforce the kind of uncomplicated sympathy typical of popular domestic tragedy. But Webster finds a way of going beyond this when Isabella 'nobly' pretends that it is her jealousy rather than Brachiano's continued adultery which is perpetuating the marital rift. The pretended fury takes

on a reality of its own and renders visible the violent passions
boiling beneath the surface of all of Webster's characters:

> To dig the strumpet's eyes out, let her lie
> Some twenty months a-dying, to cut off
> Her nose and lips, pull out her rotten teeth,
> Preserve her flesh like mummia, for trophies
> Of my just anger.
>
> (II. i. 245–9)

To hear this stream of abuse issuing from Isabella's lips is shocking in the way that the guttural oaths which come from the
possessed young girl in *The Exorcist* are shocking. The justification for such effects is the need to go beyond naturalism to
uncover aspects of the psyche normally subject to repression. In
fact, many of the non-naturalistic devices of Elizabethan drama,
such as the use of disguise, madness or 'out-of-character' behaviour, can be analysed as forms of expressionism which are
grounded in a view of human nature as violent, unstable and
contrarious. There is nothing incoherent about such a dramaturgy and, from the perspective of the late twentieth century,
little evidence to contradict its psychological assumptions.

The powerful impression of emotional truth one gets from
Webster's plays is one reason why, despite the breaches of
'realism', the complications of perspective, the absence of characters with whom one can identify, and the pervasive theatrical
self-consciousness, any comparison with Brecht is seriously misleading. Watching *The White Devil* is not a process of detached
observation in which feelings are subordinated to rational and
critical judgement. It is, rather, a disturbing and highly emotional
experience of violent chaos. The play is an assault on the sensibili-
ties of the audience, not an invitation to cool commentary. In
cinematic terms, Webster is much closer to the emotional violence of Bergman than the Brechtian tricks of Godard. Even
when Bergman does apparently make use of a Brechtian aliena-
tion device, such as the famous simulated projector breakdown
in *Persona*, the effect is emotional rather than intellectual. The
viewer is not detached from the conflicts of the characters by
being made aware of the medium of representation. Instead,
there is the terrifying sensation of being sucked into a vortex of

psychic disintegration. Webster's discontinuities serve a similar end, provoking existential anxieties rather than rational reflection.

Like Bergman, and unlike Brecht or Godard, Webster's psychological probings go hand in hand with, and can scarcely be divorced from, metaphysical questions. His characters' lives attain their full significance only in relation to death. In the terminology of Heidegger, their being-in-the-world only becomes complete when it realises itself as a being-toward-death.[6] Webster's preoccupation with death has of course been a staple topic of criticism for a long time, but it is important to be precise about the nature of this preoccupation. Eliot's famous lines ('Webster was much possessed by death / And saw the skull beneath the skin') are misleading if they are taken to suggest only a medieval brooding on universal and inevitable mortality. In fact, as Thomas McAlindon argues, 'Webster's two great tragedies show less concern with death – in the sense of mortality and decay – than they do with the art of noble dying.'[7] Like Heidegger, Webster sees the possibility of authentic being in the fact that each man or woman must face their own death in their own way. Princes may deal out deaths and punishments by the hands of others but they cannot delegate their own dying. In confronting the reality of their own immediate extinction, men and women have the chance to achieve an understanding more authentic than the commonplaces which have sustained them and their culture. When Brachiano punishes Flamineo for the murder of Marcello by leaving him under permanent sentence of death, forced to renew his lease on life day by day, he is only formalising what is already the existential situation of all the characters – and, of course, at the very moment of passing sentence his own helmet is being sprinkled with deadly poison.

The conjunction of Webster and twentieth-century existentialism should not seem surprising or arbitrary since Heidegger's thoughts on mortality and existence were developed out of rich Christian and classical traditions of philosophising about death, traditions in which Webster and his culture were saturated. Montaigne, a favourite writer of Webster's, devoted one of his essays to a consideration of the standard Renaissance view 'That to Philosophise is to learne how to Die' and wrote in another essay that the day of our death 'is the master-day, the day that judgeth all others. . . . When I judge of other men's lives, I ever respect how

they have behaved themselves in their end; and my chiefest
study is, I may well demeane my selfe at my last gaspe, that is
to say, quietly and constantly'.[8] The importance of meeting death
with calmness and dignity is usually associated with Stoic philosophy and, within Stoicism, particularly the writings of Seneca,
but it was almost equally emphasised by all the other ancient
philosophical schools influential in the Renaissance. From a
Christian perspective the overwhelming significance of the
moment of death lay more in the possibility of a last-minute repentance, something dramatised so intensely in *Doctor Faustus*.
Within Elizabethan and Jacobean Anglicanism the need to turn
to God in one's dying moments continued to be stressed despite
the coexistence of Calvinist dogmas of predestined damnation.
Writing in 1613, Thomas Tuke in *A Discourse of Death* encouraged
his readers by quoting from the Church Fathers: 'Let no man de-
spaire of pardon (saith Isidore) though he repent about the end
of his life: for God judge[s] every one as his end is, and not as
his life was.'[9] A 'good' or 'bad' death would still be important
from a Calvinist viewpoint but it would be seen less as a decisive
final choice than as a last sign of election or reprobation, the outward marker of an inescapable inner spiritual state.

Within these contexts it is easy to understand why death and
dying are given so much significance in Webster's plays. The violent, disordered lives of his characters are brought into mural
and artistic focus by the prolonged scrutiny of their endings.
However, paradoxically and unsettlingly, the many suggestions
that death is the final guarantor of meaning and authenticity are
mingled, at moments, with anticipations of the Sartrean notion
that it is death itself which renders life terrifyingly absurd and
devoid of meaning. Hints of this more negative brand of existentialism can be found in the prolonged and agonising death of
Brachiano. In the face of very strong competition, this has a good
claim to be the most horrible death in the whole of Jacobean tragedy. Spread over 175 lines, it begins with screams of physical
pain as he tears at the poisoned helmet, like Hercules with the
shirt of Nessus, and ends in spiritual torment as the friars admin-
istering the last rites reveal themselves as his murderers. His
absence from the stage between lines 41 and 83 briefly interrupts
this onslaught on the audience but only to allow articulation of
the contempt in which his followers hold him and to permit the

application of disfiguring make-up. That his appearance has changed visibly for the worse is probably indicated by the comment 'There's death in's face already' when he re-enters. Since he is the Duke himself and in the midst of his own court, the mad ravings into which he descends are more disturbing than if they came from a minor character. Like Lear's mad speeches, they carry the inescapable suggestion of a derangement at the very heart of the state, a derangement which cannot be confined to the margins of society. When Vittoria tells him his delusions are 'nothing', he replies:

> Nothing? Rare! Nothing! When I want money
> Our treasury is empty; there is nothing.
> (V. iii. 109–10)

The words are expressive of total moral and spiritual bankruptcy. In the face of death there are no resources, no reserves, for this 'great man' to draw upon. During life he acknowledged no values but the successful assertion of his own will and so death represents the absolute negation of everything which gave his existence meaning. A dead 'politician' is an absurdity and Brachiano's unappeasable fear of death is memorably expressed in an order which mocks itself:

> On pain of death, let no man name death to me,
> It is a word infinitely terrible.
> (V. iii. 39–40)

Amid the horror and confusion of his dying, there are several suggestions of significant patterning. The murderous perversion of the last rites recalls the murderous exploitation of the ritual devotions Isabella offered to her husband's picture ('*she kneels down as to prayers, then draws the curtain of the picture, does three reverences to it, and kisses it thrice*'), the link being strengthened visually by the presence of candles in both scenes. The moment of consideration Brachiano shows for Vittoria ('Do not kiss me, for I shall poison thee') recalls the dying Isabella's consideration for others ('*she faints and will not suffer them to come near it*'). Close and imaginative reading of the text can disclose further possible examples of such patterning. In order to view his wife's murder,

Brachiano is required by the conjuror to put on a charmed night-cap (II. ii. 21). In the 1981 Oxford Playhouse production, as the magic 'vision' unfolded, he clutched his hands to this cap, rolling his head from side to side as if in the grip of a convulsive fit. The full point of this became apparent in Act V when Brachiano emerged from the barriers, tearing desperately at the poisoned helmet and shaking his head in agony. All these parallelisms serve to link crime with punishment, Brachiano's terrible death with the earlier murder of his wife, thus intimating a moral significance rather than just an existential horror. The point may be that it is only a certain kind of life, the life lived by Brachiano and similar 'great men', which is negated and rendered meaningless by death. However, the intense impact of his final sufferings and the absence from the play of strongly articulated alternatives to his self-willed existence mean that it is difficult to confine the significance of his death within a neat retributive pattern. Its horror overflows beyond the individual case to confront the audience with something 'infinitely terrible'.

It is with this 'hideous storm of terror' still fresh in our minds that we are better able to appreciate the courage shown by Vittoria and Flamineo as they face their own deaths. It is not a courage rooted in moral or religious confidence but something closer to the desperate courage of an animal at bay, the courage shown by Macbeth in his last moments:

> They have tied me to the stake; I cannot fly
> But bear-like I must fight the course.

The impression of a baited bear is even stronger in the final scene of *The White Devil* since Flamineo is bound to a pillar (possibly one of the supports for the stage roof visible in the famous drawing of the Swan theatre) and subjected to the taunts of his killers. The notion of the moment of death as a moment of special authenticity is most searchingly and ambiguously dramatised in this scene. Montaigne had written (in Florio's translation), 'In all the rest there may be some maske. . . . But when that last part of our death, and of our selves comes to be acted, then no dissembling will availe, then is it high time to speake plaine English, and put off all vizards', and had supported this by quoting Lucretius:

> For then are sent true speeches from the heart,
> We are ourselves, we leave to play a part.[10]

However, he had gone on to admit that 'three of the most exe-
crable persons that ever I knew in all abomination of life' had
made a good end and, in Florio's words, there is the usual trace
of ambiguity in the word 'acted' ('when that last part of our
death. . . comes to be acted'). The murderers, Lodovico, Gasparo
and their confederates, throw off their disguises with a flourish,
but their victims, Vittoria and Flamineo (still accompanied by the
black figure of Zanche), remain enigmatic 'white devils' to the
last, because the sense of a 'performance' is never wholly absent.

In the complicated build-up to their deaths, Vittoria and
Flamineo project an extraordinary sequence of attitudes and
emotions, some of which can be seen to be deliberately deceptive
whilst others leave the audience uncertain how to respond.
Before Lodovico and Gasparo burst in, Vittoria has successively
appeared as meditatively pious (she is discovered with a devotional book in her hands), self-righteously aggressive towards
Flamineo, eloquently moralistic about the proposed suicide pact,
nobly Stoic when this seems necessary, then savagely violent
when given a chance of survival. Her brave words to her
murderers ('I shall welcome death / As princes do some great
ambassadors; / I'll meet thy weapon half way') were preceded
by very similar ones to Flamineo, uttered as part of a conscious
attempt to deceive him:

> To kill oneself is meat that we must take
> Like pills, not chew't, but quickly swallow it;
>
> (V. vi. 74–5)

Nothing in the rhetoric distinguishes the 'acted' courage from
the 'real' courage and of course, in the theatre, there can be no
such final distinction. Her bravery can in fact seem more humanly truthful if we view it not as 'natural' but as a willed
attitude, maintained with difficulty. It is preceded by futile ap-
peals to Lodovico's pity and desperate stratagems to delay the
inevitable ('If Florence be i'th' court, would he would kill me')
and is followed by manifestations of the sense of guilt which Vit-

toria could conceal from her judges but never entirely from herself:

> O my greatest sin lay in my blood.
> Now my blood pays for it.
> (V. vi. 238–9)

If her last scene is one of her greatest performances, that is not to dismiss it automatically as inauthentic. In some philosophies, a good performance in the face of death is the most to which we can aspire.

The impression of dying as a performance rather than a process of self-revelation is even stronger in the case of Flamineo. With great artistic daring Webster allows him to stage an elaborate mock-death, complete with eloquent speeches and faked symptoms of physical pain, only minutes before his real death. It is characteristic of Webster's sophisticated dramaturgy to mock a theatrical convention (in this case, the lengthy death-speech) before promptly recuperating it. When Flamineo leaps to his feet crying, 'I am not wounded: / The pistols held no bullets', it is a melodramatic twist worthy of Beaumont and Fletcher, but the shock of his actual murder within minutes of this is a much more complex emotional challenge to the audience, since his mocking laughter is not stilled by the onset of genuine catastrophe, though it is joined by a range of other attitudes. There are flashes of Stoic defiance ('We cease to grieve, cease to be Fortune's slaves, / Nay cease to die by dying'), attempts at witty pathos ('I have caught an everlasting cold'), admissions of guilt ('My life was a black charnel'), and frequent moralising couplets. The discontinuities, stylistic as well as philosophic, mean that his courage, like Vittoria's, has the air of an unstable effort of the will achieved in the face of a terrifying moral and religious void. This existential nullity is constantly being glimpsed behind the defiant poses. When his captors demand to know what he is thinking about, he replies:

> Nothing; of nothing: leave thy idle questions;
> I am i'th'way to study a long silence,
> To prate were idle; I remember nothing.
> There's nothing of so infinite vexation

As man's own thoughts.

(V. vi. 200–4)

The nothings echo emptily, recalling the mad despair of Brachiano, but the sharpest paradox may be that the very struggle to assert the self in the face of a void increases the feelings of emptiness it was intended to overcome. This self-defeating process can be clearly inferred from some of Flamineo's most famous lines:

I do not look
Who went before, nor who shall follow me;
No, at myself I will begin and end.
While we look up to heaven we confound
Knowledge with knowledge. O I am in a mist.
(V. vi. 254–8)

To look up to heaven is no longer to find religious assurance but to be plunged into a post-Reformation confusion of different philosophies and belief-systems. In the face of such confusion, Flamineo and many of the other characters in *The White Devil* turn toward the self as the sole foundation of existence only to find further confusion and emptiness, imaged by the all-pervasive mist in which they are trapped. Such a nightmarish vision of existence ('Their lives a general mist of error / Their deaths a hideous storm of terror') undoubtedly incorporates moral judgements but these are made problematic through strategies of ambiguous characterisation and subordinated to affective considerations. Again and again, we are made to *feel* the violence, confusion and horror of this existence, and to feel also some of the paradoxical value of this relentless self-assertion in the face of death. Nietzsche saw that, in the absence of moral and religious foundations, existence could only be justified aesthetically and there is undoubtedly some feeling of aesthetic success, however partial and provisional, in the last performances of Vittoria and Flamineo; as there is also of course, quite openly, in the sinister boasting of Lodovico, who may well be articulating Webster's own satisfaction with his hard-won achievement:

I limb'd this night-piece and it was my best.

4
The Duchess of Malfi

Webster's second tragedy repeats and reworks many of the situations, themes, characters, images and even individual lines from *The White Devil*. Once more we find ourselves in a sixteenth-century Italian court where the ruthlessness of great men and the corrupt authority of the Catholic church – a linkage vividly dramatised by the Cardinal's exchange of his ecclesiastical robes for armour – combine to crush any possibilities of healthy or honest existence. Once more there is the close scrutiny of how men and women meet their deaths, as if only in their final extremity can their value be truly known. The similarities between the two plays are such that many critical generalisations about Webster fail to make any real distinction between his two masterpieces. Yet any analysis should begin by acknowledging the much greater emotional range of *The Duchess of Malfi*, a difference largely brought about by the introduction of a protagonist with whom the audience can more easily sympathise. The explosive cynicism and violence of *The White Devil* is still present but is now counterpointed with scenes of romantic and domestic intimacy, whose impact is deepened by their elegiac tone. The character of the Duchess brings the play much closer to commonly perceived norms of tragedy, whether Shakespearean or Aristotelian. Terror is now conjoined with pity (a word used much more frequently than in *The White Devil*).

The difference between the two plays emerges clearly in the different strategy of characterisation adopted. Whilst there is an equivalent complexity of treatment in *The Duchess of Malfi*, it is not grounded, except perhaps in the case of Bosola, in a general premise of radical moral paradox. It is not easy to 'read' people in this play (Antonio's boast to Bosola, 'I do understand your inside', is greeted with a contemptuous 'Do you so?') but there is a much stronger impression of a core of moral and psychological identity beneath the surface 'contradictions'. Rather than make each of his characters a 'white devil', Webster seems to have started with a groundplan based on the four personality types of Elizabethan humour psychology, a procedure also followed by Shakespeare in *Julius Caesar*.[1] To say that Webster initially saw the Duchess as corresponding to the sanguine type, Ferdinand to the choleric, the Cardinal to the phlegmatic, and Bosola to the melancholic, tells us little about the final effects achieved but does suggest a desire for strong dramatic contrasts based on clearly distinct personalities. The imposition of a homogenous overall design by a director, as was done by Philip Prowse for the National Theatre in 1985, can flatten these differences, robbing the play of a good deal of its real life and leaving the audience with 'the sensation of watching a lot of interchangeable black figures scurrying about inside a beautifully-lit glass jar'.[2] The Duchess and her brothers may be 'cast in one figure' but they are of entirely 'different temper' and the staging should enforce this. Likewise, Bosola's status as a malcontent is better registered if he alone, rather than the whole cast, is dressed in black. After his 'promotion' to the provisorship of the horse he is told by Ferdinand 'Keep your old garb of melancholy', and it seems likely that he remains dressed in black throughout, a costuming equally appropriate to his later roles of tomb-maker and revenger.

The *Duchess of Malfi* is not a play which radically challenges the supposition of a coherent and continuous personal identity, but it does suggest emotional complexities and depths of a kind unusual in the theatre outside the works of Shakespeare. The dominant impression is not of unresolvable psychological discontinuities but of secret inner lives which can only be excavated at great cost to all concerned. Ferdinand threatens the Duchess:

> Your darkest actions: nay, your privat'st thoughts,
> Will come to light.
>
> > (I. ii. 238–9)

but he recoils from what he finds in both her and himself:

> Curse upon her!
> I will no longer study in the book
> Of another's heart:
>
> > (IV. i. 15–17)

and the knowledge destroys them both. Bosola's strenuous efforts to uncover the Duchess's secrets mirror the endeavours of the audience to penetrate the façades of characters whose mysterious inner selves are constantly being hinted at. The Cardinal seems to have the energetic worldliness which Webster's contemporaries saw as typical of Italian Renaissance Catholicism:

> They say he's a brave fellow, will play his five thousand crowns at tennis, dance, court ladies, and one that hath fought single combats. (I. ii. 76–9)

But these are only 'flashes' which 'superficially hang on him, for form'. His 'inward character' has a cold and joyless emptiness which seems closer to the monkish vice of accidie than to the sensuality and ruthlessness of the Borgia popes. The particular challenge of this role for an actor is to allow this despairing blankness to show through enough to modify an otherwise potentially two-dimensional picture of Machiavellian villainy. Similarly, what appears mirth in Ferdinand 'is merely outside'. When he first enters, surrounded by his courtiers, he seems a typical enough Renaissance prince, suavely conversing of horsemanship and war. Then some laughter at a sexual innuendo provokes him into an outburst which shatters the flow of aristocratic banter:

> Why do you laugh? Methinks you that are my courtiers should be my touchwood, take fire when I give fire; that is, laugh when I laugh, were the subject never so witty –
>
> > (I. ii. 43–6)

In the theatre these lines are usually succeeded by a strained silence (Webster's concluding dash may be a way of marking this pause), a silence broken sometimes by a sinister chuckle from Ferdinand himself as the cue for the resumption of merriment. With great dramatic economy, Webster has suggested turbulences and instabilities, perhaps of a sexual nature, beneath the surface courtliness and hinted at how terrifying such hidden disturbances might become when combined with despotic power.

In a play of many secrets, Ferdinand's dark and twisted sexuality is the most secret thing of all, unremarked upon by any character in the play, including Ferdinand himself. The reluctance of some critics to accept that his relationship with the Duchess is contaminated by unconscious incestuous attraction is understandable given the absurd excesses which have often accompanied psychoanalytic criticism and the general rarity of unacknowledged motives in Elizabethan and Jacobean drama. Even at its most sophisticated, it was a drama of expressive plenitude rather than one of implication and subtext, and it is hard to think of many comparably compelling examples of unexplained feelings. One, perhaps, would be the mysterious melancholy voiced by Antonio at the beginning of *The Merchant of Venice* ('In sooth I know not why I am so sad'). This creates an immediate puzzle for the audience which is never resolved explicitly but whose solution, as in the case of Ferdinand, requires the inference of a 'love that dare not speak its name'. Webster may have had this example in mind since he repeats Shakespeare's unusual tactic of deliberately foregrounding a psychological problem which he does not intend to clear up:

FERDINAND: . . . she's a young widow,
    I would not have her marry again.
BOSOLA: No, sir?
FERDINAND: Do not you ask the reason: but be satisfied,
    I say I would not.

                                (I. ii. 179–82)

The point of this exchange is surely to leave the audience very much *un*satisfied and to stimulate the kind of search for small behavioural clues frequently expected of modern audiences but less usual in the Jacobean theatre. Such clues are found in the in-

appropriate erotic tone which colours Ferdinand's interchanges
with his sister ('Farewell, lusty widow'), the hysterical fury with
which he imagines her in 'the very act of sin' with a succession
of imaginary lovers, and the emotional violence which dissolves
his unconvincing attempts at rationalisation into syntactical
chaos:

> For let me but examine well the cause;
> What was the meaning of her match to me?
> Only I must confess, I had a hope,
> Had she continu'd widow to have gain'd
> An infinite mass of treasure by her death:
> And that was the main cause; her marriage,
> That drew a stream of gall quite through my heart;
>
> (IV. ii. 279–85)

The textual evidence, although subtle, is collectively overwhelming and, despite the long critical tradition of arguing that
Webster's characterisation is casual and incoherent, the danger
for a modern director lies less in ignoring this subtext than in
giving it vulgar overemphasis of the kind common in Freudian
treatments of the Hamlet–Gertrude relationship. In a recent
French adaptation of *The Duchess of Malfi*, Ferdinand planted a
fish impaled on a knife between his sister's thighs.[3] With stage
business like this it is difficult to sustain the peculiar atmosphere
of this play, an atmosphere heavy with the secrecy of thoughts
and feelings not known fully even to their possessors.

The always difficult and technically demanding process of ex-
position whereby we are introduced to the major characters and
their relationships is handled with particular brilliance in *The
Duchess of Malfi*. The first act takes the form of one continuous
flowing scene, mixing formal commentary with naturalistic interchanges, and constantly shuffling and recombining the main
figures into different groupings. We see Bosola with the Cardinal,
the Cardinal with Ferdinand, the Duchess with both her brothers, the Duchess alone with Ferdinand, the Duchess alone with
Antonio. The stage is never cleared of actors (so the introduction
of a scene division by D. C. Gunby in the Penguin edition has no
authority) but seems to shift from a crowded open court to the
intimacy of the Duchess's private chamber. This kind of fluid,

though strictly 'illogical' transition is always possible in a theatre
where locations are established by the words of the actors rather
than scenery. The effect of this kaleidoscopic pattern of interac-
tions, mixed in with commentary from Delio, Antonio and
Bosola, is extremely complex, much more so than, for instance,
the opening of *The Revenger's Tragedy*, where the court are
straightforwardly paraded as objects of disgust before the satirical gaze of Vindice. In Webster's play, too, we are continually
prompted to make judgements but these are of a very provisional nature and subject to constant modification, as we match
one comment against another and both against an unfolding
sequence of actions, a process which goes on through the play.

Nowhere is this process of adjustment more evident than in
the case of Bosola. As ex-convict, spy, gaoler, comforter, executioner and penitent avenger, he presents special difficulties for
audience and actor alike. His subsequent moral gyrations are
carefully prepared for by two early pieces of commentary from
Antonio (already given some interpretive authority by his opening speech on the French court). In the first few minutes of a play
the audience is particularly anxious to get its bearings and is
gratefully attentive to speeches such as the following:

> Here comes Bosola
> The only court-gall: yet I observe his railing
> Is not for simple love of piety:
> Indeed he rails at those things which he wants,
> Would be as lecherous, covetous, or proud,
> Bloody, or envious, as any man,
> If he had means to be so.
>
> (I. i. 22–8)

Bosola's cynicism is given the most cynical gloss possible and his
character is comfortably assimilated to a type familiar from previous satirical drama and literature. Hence it is unsettling, in the
way that much of *The White Devil* is unsettling, when only fifty
lines later Antonio himself provides a very different perspective:

> 'Tis great pity
> He should be thus neglected, I have heard

> He's very valiant. This foul melancholy
> Will poison all his goodness. . .
>
> (I. i. 73–6)

Since Webster constructed Bosola's part by combining several
different figures from his sources and since disguise is used (as
in many Renaissance plays) to extend his dramatic functions beyond the limits of what is humanly plausible, it may seem
irrelevant to probe the question of his 'character' too deeply. Yet
theatre history indicates that in the most highly praised productions of *The Duchess of Malfi* (the Haymarket in 1945 and the
Manchester Royal Exchange in 1980) Cecil Trouncer and Bob
Hoskins succeeded in making sense of the part and projecting an
all-too-human suffering and anguish. Some forms of drama can
indeed dispense with the concept of character but not plays
which hope to move pity as well as terror in an audience.

In fact Bosola seems less puzzling as soon as one realises that
he is an inhabitant of what Primo Levi, writing of Auschwitz,
called 'The Grey Zone', that space in which the distinction between guard and prisoner, oppressor and victim, starts to break
down. Levi quotes a survivor of the 'Special Squad' of prisoners
who helped the Germans operate the crematoria at Auschwitz as
saying: 'You mustn't think that we are monsters; we are the same
as you, only much more unhappy.'[4] Bosola, driven by his pov-
erty, does not have the moral or material strength to resist the
murderous orders of his masters, but he can never wholly extin-
guish his conscience and so is filled with a corrosive self-hatred.
His continued capacity to feel pity, which so surprises Ferdinand
('Thy pity is nothing of kin to thee'), would not have surprised
Primo Levi. Recording an incident in which members of the
'Special Squad' tried to save a young woman who had miraculously revived after the gassing, he wrote: 'Compassion and
brutality can coexist in the same individual and in the same
moment, despite all logic; and for all that compassion itself
eludes logic.'[5] This seems a more appropriate way of approaching the problem of Bosola, as it presents itself in the theatre, than
that of treating him semiotically as a mobile signifier, without
depth or human truth.

The constant modification of provisional judgements takes
place in relation to the Duchess as well as Bosola. It quickly be-

comes apparent that she is both more and less than the plaster saint of Antonio's initial encomium, a speech which, in the Manchester Royal Exchange production, was delivered with the actors 'frozen' and a spotlight on the Duchess, increasing the iconic effect:

> in that look
> There speaketh so divine a continence,
> As cuts off all lascivious, and vain hope.
> Her days are practis'd in such noble virtue,
> That, sure her nights, nay more, her very sleeps,
> Are more in heaven, than other ladies' shrifts.
>
> (I. ii. 123–8)

Within minutes she shows herself to be no 'figure cut in alabaster' but a passionate and spirited woman whose desire to love and be loved is stronger than any fear of her menacing brothers. Her defiance of them may be rash ('it shows / A fearful madness') but it springs from an essential innocence, 'the innocence of abundant life in a sick and melancholy society, where the fact that she has "youth and a little beauty" is precisely why she is hated'.[6] No twentieth-century production has succeeded in making her unsympathetic, though crude forms of historical criticism continue to attempt this feat. Well-documented Renaissance social prejudices against widows remarrying (seen in the bitter line from *Hamlet*, 'None wed the second but who killed the first') and against alliances that cross class barriers are cited to 'prove' that Jacobean audiences must have seen the Duchess as seriously blameworthy in marrying her steward. Such arguments ignore the way major literature works against as well as within prevailing ideologies, especially when these are not wholly determinant of social practice (it was normal for young widows to remarry and not unknown for great ladies to marry beneath themselves), and are no more convincing when given a modern feminist twist than they were as part of older versions of historical criticism. According to Lisa Jardine, Ferdinand's ravings about his sister's 'looseness' take on special authority because 'only men surround the Duchess; the audience can do little more than accept their version of her behaviour and motives'.[7] On this reading, the moment she marries Antonio she is transformed into a 'lascivi-

ous whore. It is not merely that her brothers see her as such; the
dominant strain in the subsequent representation is such.'[8] This
account seems to posit an intellectually inert audience who are
unable to perceive a meaningful contrast between what is said
about a character and how she or he actually behaves (a distinction central to any complex dramaturgy) and who are unable to
feel a moral and emotional preference for love and tenderness
when these are set against violent perversity.

Contrary to what Jardine says, the 'dominant strain' in the
representation of the Duchess, prior to the roles of prisoner and
martyr thrust upon her in Act IV, is that of lover, wife and
mother. Much of the emotional effect of the play derives from its
intimation of how precarious personal and domestic happiness
are, how vulnerable to tyrannical violence and to the exigencies
of life in general. When Delio asks, 'How fares it with the Duchess?' and is told by Antonio, 'She's expos'd / Unto the worst of
torture, pain, and fear' (II. iii. 65–6), the lines anticipate her sufferings in prison but their immediate reference is to the labour
of childbirth. Quietly embedded beneath the play's surface conflicts are the successive stages of a woman's life-journey through
courtship, marriage and childbirth, to ageing, parting and death.
Within this sequence there are many moments of gaiety, love and
laughter but the underlying pressure of time and mortality is always felt, constantly suggesting an inescapable sadness at the
heart of existence. The wooing of Antonio takes place whilst the
Duchess draws up her will and the language of love is inflected
with imagery of death. The laughter of the bedchamber scene ('I
prithee / When were we so merry?') is quickly followed by the
first fears of ageing ('Doth not the colour of my hair 'gin to
change?'). Different interpretations of a play as complex as *The
Duchess of Malfi* will always tend to bring different scenes into
prominence but evidence drawn from actual performances
should carry a particular weight. After the prison scenes of Act
IV (seen as crucial in virtually every account of the play), it is remarkable how often theatre critics have singled out the wooing
scene and the bedchamber scene for special praise, often commending as well the scene of parting near Ancona and the echo
scene. These are episodes of extraordinary emotional delicacy
whose impact in the theatre is out of all proportion to their
length, and which make it impossible to classify the play as a

'tragical satire' that takes its dominant tone from Bosola's cynicism. Even in Peter Gill's Brechtian production for the Royal Court in 1971, the scenes between Antonio and the Duchess carried a special charge as the actors responded to the nuances of Webster's language, at once naturalistic and poetic, to rise above the uniform and distancing bleakness of the chosen production style.

It has become commonplace in Marxist and feminist analyses of society and literature to see personal relations and family life as reproducing and enforcing oppressive political structures rather than opposing them or creating a free emotional space. For Althusser, the celebrated French Marxist philosopher and wife murderer, the family was 'the most terrible, unbearable, and frightening of all Ideological Apparatuses of the State'. Yet those tyrannies with genuinely totalitarian ambitions (such as the regimes of Hitler, Stalin and Mao) have consistently viewed domestic loves and loyalties as threateningly independent of state power and a source of potential resistance. The extensive theorisation of the family as a source of oppression dwindles into insignificance when confronted with the actuality of state violence against the family. The scene on the road near Ancona – the little family group clutching a few possessions and confronted by armed men – awakens memories of a hundred newsreels and no doubt had a similar emotional impact on seventeenth-century audiences who were not ignorant of the effects of war and tyranny on domestic happiness. With some naïvety, given the nature of her brothers, the Duchess had hoped to create a secure circle of personal happiness for herself and Antonio:

> All discord, without this circumference,
> Is only to be pitied, and not fear'd.
> (I. ii. 387–8)

She fails tragically but her struggle is not thereby stripped of its emotional and moral value nor does her secret family life cease to suggest a powerful alternative to the diseased world of the court.

The moment when this dimension of the play, together with much else, comes most sharply into dramatic focus is probably the bedchamber scene. The atmosphere of domestic cosiness, often increased by the presence of children's toys onstage (a concretisation of such allusions as 'I have seen my little boy oft scourge his top'), coexists from the beginning with a sense of menace which becomes horribly palpable when Ferdinand approaches his sister unseen. The stage picture of the Duchess brushing her hair before a mirror whilst her brother advances from behind with a dagger has a raw melodramatic force, but it also carries a wealth of iconographic significance, some of it possibly self-contradictory. For Keith Sturgess, 'a Renaissance moral emblem of shattering power is achieved: the vain woman, her vanity symbolised by the mirror, visited by Death as a retribution for a moral laxity of which the play never acquits her'.[9] However, it is always possible to interpret such a tableau less moralistically and more lyrically and wistfully, seeing the woman's long hair as a potently sensuous image of the preciousness of life, youth and beauty in the face of death, time and barely guessed at horrors. Some such archetypal opposition is involved in the famous lines from *The Waste Land*:

> A woman drew her long black hair out tight
> And fiddled whisper music on those strings
> And bats with baby faces in the violet light
> Whistled, and beat their wings
> And crawled head downward down a blackened wall . . .[10]

An equally potent modern rendering of the primal opposition which shapes Webster's scene is Gustav Klimt's painting *Death and Life*, in which a lovingly interlocked family group (stylised to resemble a patterned quilt) is menaced by a sinister skull-figure wielding a club. Conjunctions of death and life in Renaissance art and literature frequently manage to combine, as in Webster's tableau, a 'medieval' sense of life's vanity with a more 'modern' sense of life's irreplaceable value. Moreover, any allegorical reading of this scene would have to acknowledge that Ferdinand suggests the Devil as much as he does Death. When he hands the Duchess a dagger, the implication is that he is tempting her to suicide rather than simply threatening her with murder:

DUCHESS: He left this with me.
She shows the poniard.

ANTONIO: And it seems, did wish
   You would use it on yourself?
DUCHESS: His action seem'd
   To intend so much.

                                    (III. ii. 150–2)

With this gesture Ferdinand aligns himself with the diabolical agents of the morality plays whose attempts to damn the Mankind figure frequently culminated in a temptation to that final despair of God's mercy which suicide was thought to indicate (a convention followed also in *Doctor Faustus* when Mephostophilis hands Faustus a dagger near the climax of the play).[11] In his obsessive and destructive opposition to the Duchess's marriage, Ferdinand does indeed sometimes resemble Shakespeare's demi-devil Iago, whilst anticipating the lonely, jealous agony of Milton's Satan when confronted with the married bliss of Adam and Eve:

> Sight hateful, sight tormenting! thus these two
> Imparadised in one another's arms,
> The happier Eden, shall enjoy their fill
> Of bliss on bliss, while I to hell am thrust.[12]

The devilish aspect of Ferdinand is not something which appears momentarily and casually in the bedchamber scene. It is a consistent motif in the play, sustained by patterns of verbal imagery and pieces of stage business. The interpretation of his actions put forward above by Antonio and the Duchess should cause us to rethink the significance of that earlier moment when Ferdinand presented his sister with a dagger:

> You are my sister,
> This was my father's poniard: do you see,
> I'ld be loath to see't look rusty, 'cause 'twas his.
>   (I. ii. 252–3)

As well as the more obvious implications of murderous threat, offended family honour and disturbed sexuality (the latter heightened by the intimacy of the moment since it is the first time Ferdinand and the Duchess are seen alone together), we should probably be aware of an emblematic aspect, derived from morality play representations of the temptation to despair. A modern director, by such devices as getting Ferdinand to finger his weapon suggestively, is more likely to emphasise the sexual dimension to the exclusion of all else and, indeed, Webster often seems to aim for more significance than any particular performance is capable of encompassing. However, the diabolic persecution of Act IV ('Why do you do this?', 'To bring her to despair') is most dramatically effective when viewed as part of a larger pattern of meaning which has been built into the play from the very beginning and which can be glimpsed in the smallest of gestures.

Carefully prepared for in the three previous acts, the scenes of suffering and death in the prison (once the Duchess's palace) are unmatched in English drama for their relentless intensity. Their non-naturalistic 'excesses' (the dead man's hand, the waxwork figures and the masque of madmen) have provoked some of the most hostile criticism ever directed at a major dramatist (including Shaw's famous gibe at Webster as the 'Tussaud laureate') but I have yet to see a production in which these scenes were ever less than wholly compelling. If there are problems with Webster's play, they are to be found in the fifth act rather than the fourth. The triangle of relationships between Bosola, Ferdinand and the Duchess is developed with such moral and emotional intensity that Webster is able to move from full-blown symbolic and poetic effects to touches of intimate naturalism without ever losing his grip on the essential psychology of his situations. The grotesque trick with the dead man's hand (with its hints of diabolism and witchcraft) is accompanied by the simple, misplaced compassion of 'You are very cold. / I fear you are not well after your travel' (IV. i. 51–2). The surreal, dreamlike poetry with which the Duchess expresses her indifference to the means of execution can modulate suddenly into a burst of all-too-human irritation at the whispered preparations going on around her:

> What would it pleasure me, to have my throat cut
> With diamonds? or to be smothered
> With cassia? or to be shot to death, with pearls?
> I know death hath ten thousand several doors
> For men to take their exits: and 'tis found

They go on such strange geometrical hinges,
You may open them both ways: any way, for Heaven
   sake,
So I were out of your whispering.

(IV. ii. 216–23)

The diamonds, cassia and pearls form part of an elaborate and
justly admired network of recurrent verbal images, but the suddenly contextualised immediacy of the final phrase is what
shows Webster to be a great *dramatic* poet.

Much of Act IV is indeed highly ritualistic rather than naturalistic in form and where there are traceable sources for the
details of the Duchess's ordeal, these tend to be literary rather
than historical. But it is easy to exaggerate the distance between
poetic art and life. Jacobean audiences might well have been reminded of the actual plight of Lady Arabella Stuart, cousin to
James I, whose secret marriage to William Seymour aroused the
anger of the king. The lovers attempted to flee to Europe but
only Seymour succeeded in reaching Ostend. Arabella was captured at sea and brought back to be imprisoned in the Tower,
where she went mad from grief. Modern audiences, lacking
such an immediate political context, are nevertheless readily
drawn into intense participation in the human conflict between
tormented persecutor, suffering victim and self-divided go-
between. Some of Webster's theatrical symbolism (such as the
parodic evocation of a wedding masque) requires elucidation by
modern scholarship, but much of it, revolving as it does around
the immutable reality of death, remains immediately intelligible.
When Bosola, disguised as an old man, speaks of grey hairs and
the frailty of the flesh, he speaks to all audiences, past and present. The impersonal, choric quality of some of his speeches does
not rob them of their contextual edge since they form a crucial
part of the moral and spiritual 'testing' of the Duchess, a testing
whose outcome is made to seem more important than anything
else in the play.

These prison scenes represent Webster's most eloquent and
extended exploration of the notion, common in both Christian
and classical teaching, that in suffering and death we find the
touchstones of human value. In the opening scene of *The White*

Devil, Antonelli had attempted to comfort the banished Lodovico by drawing attention to this Renaissance commonplace:

> Perfumes the more they are chaf'd the more they render
> Their pleasing scents, and so affliction
> Expresseth virtue, fully, whether true,
> Or else adulterate.
>
> (I. i. 47–50)

In a manner typical of the earlier play, this reassuring *sententia* is scornfully rejected ('Leave your painted comforts') and super-seded by threats of violence. In *The Duchess of Malfi*, however, Webster commits himself more wholeheartedly and unambigu-ously to pursuing the dramatic possibilities of this belief. Up to a point his basic strategy resembles that of Shakespeare in *Titus Andronicus* and *King Lear*, or Kyd in *The Spanish Tragedy* – that of heaping a series of disasters upon the protagonist until grief cracks the foundations of personality producing a disintegration into madness. The masque of madmen, whatever else it might accomplish, powerfully projects this possibility but, of course, the crucial point is that the Duchess, though brought to the very brink, does not disintegrate. The pressures upon her identity ('Who am I?', 'Am I not thy Duchess?') are resisted initially by an aristocratic and Stoic assertion of self, described by Ferdinand as 'a strange disdain', which crystallises in the famous 'I am Duchess of Malfi still' (IV. ii. 141). The full resonance of this line requires a recognition of how precarious as well as forceful an assertion it is. The dominant meaning of 'still' may be that of 'constantly' or 'always' (Elizabeth I's motto was 'Semper eadem' – 'Always the same') but the weaker sense of 'yet', 'for the moment', creates an undercurrent of provisionality which is increased by the fact that a title is being used to signify personal identity, a title which can easily come to seem 'but a bare name, / And no essential thing'. Aristocratic pride helps save the Duch-ess from despair but, in the face of Bosola's relentless emphasis on mortality, it gives way to something less assertive though equally heroic – the stance of the martyr.

The Duchess indirectly confirms her assimilation to this arche-type when she hopes vainly that heaven will 'a little while, cease crowning martyrs' to punish her brothers. After the Bible, no book exerted more influence on the Protestant imagination of this period, shaping its structures of feeling, than Foxe's *Acts and Monuments*, with its massively detailed accounts (with accompanying woodcuts) of the thousands of noble deaths endured by Christians (and, latterly, Protestants) for their faith. Webster and Dekker, when writing *Sir Thomas Wyatt*, had turned to Foxe for some of the details of Lady Jane Grey's death, and would have found there some classic articulations of the difficult middle path between pride and despair which a Christian faced with death is required to tread. In her affliction, Lady Jane had prayed 'that I may neyther be too much puffed up with prosperitie, neither too much pressed down wyth adversitie: least I beeyng too full, should denie thee my GOD, or beeyng too lowe brought, should despayre and blaspheme thee my Lord and Saviour'.[13] The Duchess swings between nihilistic despair ('I could curse the stars') and the aristocratic confidence of 'I am Duchess of Malfi still', before attaining, with help from Bosola which may be partly unconscious, the calm humility of a martyr's death.

> Pull, and pull strongly, for your able strength
> Must pull down heaven upon me:
> Yet stay, heaven gates are not so highly arch'd
> As princes' palaces: they that enter there
> Must go upon their knees.
>
> (IV. ii. 230–4)

As she drops to her knees we are probably meant to recall the moment when she lifted Antonio up from his knees to bring him level with her 'greatness'. If such a visual echo seems too harshly didactic in its implications we should also recall how the Duchess and Antonio knelt together to perform their secret marriage and remember her words at Ancona: 'In the eternal Church, sir, / I do hope we shall not part thus' (III. v. 68–9).

The moral and emotional impact of the Duchess's death depends a great deal on the special value attached to martyrdom in Christian teaching but, within the context of Webster's play, its full significance is less easy to describe. As in *King Lear*, we are forced to recognise the possibility that the value we see in certain ways of living and dying has no metaphysical sanction. The Duchess dies nobly but there is no evidence that her fate dis-

turbs the universe in any way ('Look you, the stars shine still').
Moreover, faced with the mass slaughter of innocents in the
twentieth century, it has become more difficult, even perhaps of-
fensive, to continue to look for and assert a moral or religious
value in suffering. From one point of view, Auschwitz marked
the end of all such theodicy. Yet, as Emmanuel Levinas has argued, the perception of suffering as something useless and
devoid of meaning, unrationalisable, may be the step to realising
its full moral significance in the compassion and sense of injustice it arouses in others.[14]

Webster, of course, dramatises this process explicitly in the
growing emotional involvement of Bosola with his prisoner. His
refusal to appear before her undisguised after the 'cruel lie' of
the waxwork bodies is at one level a 'device' to extend the symbolic possibilities of his role, but it also has an emotional truth
rooted in his increased pity for the Duchess and growing self-
hatred. The bond between the two characters is quietly implied
by the Duchess's choice of simile to describe her suffering:

> I am acquainted with sad misery,
> As the tann'd galley-slave is with his oar.
>					(IV. ii. 27–8)

Although these lines are spoken out of Bosola's hearing, they
help to explain the painful sense of kinship felt by the ex-
prisoner in the galleys for the woman he is guarding. This compassion reaches a focal point at the moment of her brief 'revival',
a moment of great dramatic intensity which arguably surpasses
its model in *Othello*:

> She stirs; here's life.
> Return, fair soul, from darkness, and lead mine
> Out of this sensible hell. She's warm, she breathes:
> Upon thy pale lips I will melt my heart
> To store them with fresh colour. Who's there?
> Some cordial drink!
>					(IV. ii. 339–44)

It is in the nature of Webster's art, however, that uncomplicated
primary emotions are not sustained beyond a certain point, be-

ing quickly overlaid with ironies and qualifications. The existential trap closes again round Bosola, preventing his feelings being translated into saving actions ('Alas! I dare not call: / So pity would destroy pity'). Moreover, it was only after being refused his reward by Ferdinand that his change of heart became fully articulate. His sense of injustice is a strange compound of compassion and self-interest, which means that, while he becomes a channel for the powerful feelings of moral outrage engendered by the Duchess's death, we never cease to judge him.

The undeniable sense of value and significance emerging from the events of Act IV is subjected to severe challenges in Act V. A recognisably Shakespearean tragic affirmation is succeeded by scenes of violent confusion which at times seem closer to the black comedy of modern 'absurd' theatre than to conventional notions of the tragic. Figures cross a darkened stage, muttering mad and murderous thoughts. Men are struck down by accident in 'Such a mistake as I have often seen / In a play'. Every director has to take firm decisions about where audience laughter is desirable and where it must be avoided at all costs. The 1989 RSC production at the Swan was criticised, like many of its predecessors, for giving 'insufficient guidance about where laughter is legitimate'[15] and some reviewers were inclined to blame the play rather than its direction: 'Nothing can prevent its final scene from appearing highly risible to a modern audience'.[16] The simple empirical refutation of this last claim is that major productions this century (such as Adrian Noble's at Manchester in 1980) have managed to stage the last scene in such a way as to leave the audience stunned rather than tittering. The most difficult moment is always when the mad Ferdinand enters to join the struggle between Bosola and the Cardinal. It was partly the excellence of Mike Gwilym's acting which made this scuffle seem terrifying rather than merely ludicrous (he had succeeded in establishing a real continuity between Ferdinand's mad behaviour and his earlier signs of instability), but another important factor was Noble's decision to put Gwilym in modern hospital clothes. This authoritative and sobering sign of 'real' insanity made it more difficult to maintain an amused distance from his wild behaviour, as the clinical whiteness of his garments was flecked with blood.

Laughter or terror in the face of meaningless violence are by no means the only reponses prompted by the last act of Webster's play. There is also a counter-movement in the fragile but persistent and poignant sense of the Duchess's continued presence. In early 1625, Webster contributed some verses to an engraving of James I and his family. In this picture James is shown flanked by his dead wife, Queen Anne, and his dead son, Prince Henry, each bearing a skull, as well as by all his important living relatives.[17] The picture does not simply act as a *memento mori* reminding us that in the midst of life we are in death; it also asserts the importance and life of the dead, their continuing place in the world of the living. Bosola remains haunted by the Duchess, the dying Ferdinand's thoughts return obsessively to his sister, and Antonio hears the melancholy echo that issues from his wife's grave. The location of this immensely effective scene, a fort built on the ruins of an ancient abbey, simultaneously and paradoxically insists both on the mutability of life and the persistence of the past, reminding a Jacobean audience of the 'bare ruined choirs' to be found all over post-Reformation England. It is only when Antonio refuses to converse with the echo on the grounds that it is 'a dead thing' that his own fate seems to be sealed. The vision of his wife which follows ('on the sudden, a clear light / Presented me a face folded in sorrow') may well have involved the kind of primitive lighting effect which became possible in the indoor Blackfriars but remains very moving even when staged as only his 'fancy'. These moments have a considerable cumulative impact and they were taken further by Philip Prowse in 1985 when he caused the Duchess's ghost to remain onstage throughout the last act. Reviewers were divided about the effects of this but the objection that it was inconsistent with Webster's view of death as 'a black void'[18] seems misplaced. The sense of communion between the living and the dead is very strong in his plays, even if the precise nature of any 'other world' is left in doubt. The power of the echo scene is itself enough to challenge and ironise Bosola's despairing conclusion:

> We are only like dead walls, or vaulted graves
> That, ruin'd, yields no echo.
>
> (V. v. 97–8)

The felt presence of the Duchess in Act V does much to vindicate Webster's closing couplet, the most memorable of the many *sententiae* which adorn his plays:

> *Integrity of life is fame's best friend,*
> *Which nobly, beyond death, shall crown the end.*
>
> (V. v. 120–1)

However, whether visibly onstage or not, the Duchess was powerless to save her husband or avert the final bloodbath. In immediate and practical terms all hope for social and moral renewal comes to rest on Antonio's young son, brought on by Delio at the end of the play. Delio speaks confidently of 'this young hopeful gentleman' but we may remember with unease that there is another claimant to the dukedom, a son by the Duchess's first husband, and that the horoscope for Antonio's firstborn predicted a 'short life' and 'a violent death'. In thus undercutting his ending Webster may have been thinking of the recent death of Prince Henry, which had robbed critics of James's rule of their best hope for the future. The uncertainties awaiting Antonio's son were dramatised with great economy in the last few moments of Adrian Noble's production. Standing centre-stage and surrounded by courtiers, the young boy had every man kneel to him in turn before suddenly casting his gaze upward towards the inscrutable stars, the stars which had looked down calmly on his mother's death. It was a fitting conclusion to a play which, no less than *King Lear*, provokes anguished questioning rather than simply a feeling of blank hopelessness.

5

The Devil's Law-Case

As the only other surviving play of Webster's sole authorship, *The Devil's Law-Case* has had to carry a burden of critical expectation which it has scarcely been able to fulfil. Written soon after the great tragedies, it is filled with verbal, visual and situational echoes of the earlier plays but has often been described in terms reminiscent of Donne's insulting 'compliment' to a woman:

> Though all her parts be not in th'usuall place,
> She'hath yet an Anagram of a good face.[1]

All the ingredients may be excellent in themselves but they are not combined in a way which could be called pleasing. The surviving evidence suggests that Webster himself thought highly of his play, regarding it as serious literature rather than a piece of commercial hack-work. In the dedication to Sir Thomas Finch, he implies that it is of similar standard to *The White Devil*, *The Duchess of Malfi* and the lost *Guise*. The dedication is then followed by an aggressively Jonsonian note 'To the Judicious Reader' which makes clear that the play is a learned 'poem' and therefore aimed chiefly at 'the judicious'. The note ends with a Horatian tag which translates as 'I do not seek the applause of the fickle populace.' Behind this lofty tone one may, as in the Preface to *The White Devil*, detect a defensive reaction to a failure in actual performance, but the least a modern reader can do is to take Webster at his word and begin by treating his play seriously, whatever judgement on it is finally reached.

Unlike the other plays dealt with at length in this book, *The Devil's Law-Case* is formally a tragicomedy rather than a tragedy and discussion of it should begin by asking what sort of difference this makes in terms of audience involvement and expectations.[2] Are we promised that the emotional responses of pity and terror which threaten to overwhelm our 'safe' distance from what we are watching will be checked and controlled by frequent laughter and the sense of security found in the anticipated happy ending? Or that the rapid alternation of perspectives, seeing the same events now as horrific, now as laughable, will unsettle all moral and intellectual standpoints in a way which goes beyond the 'comforting' assurances of tragedy? Historically, the concept of tragicomedy has proved loose enough to embrace both *The Winter's Tale* and *Waiting for Godot*, and even when considered purely in Renaissance terms it covers a wide range of dramatic practice.

From a narrowly neoclassical standpoint, virtually all Elizabethan and Jacobean plays are of a 'mixed' kind in their mingling of tones and social classes. Medieval drama had not conformed to classical concepts of tragedy and comedy, and the roots of Elizabethan popular theatre are arguably more medieval than classical. Moreover, even when more distinct notions of dramatic genre were formulated in the sixteenth century, they were subject to constant pressure and erosion from the romantic and pastoral literary forms which were incorporated into the theatre. In the early seventeenth century the casual mingling of forms which had characterised earlier popular theatre (the title page of *Cambises* declares it to be 'a Lamentable Tragedy, mixed full of pleasant mirth') began to be superseded by a more self-conscious approach to tragicomedy. Marston's satirical plays for the reformed children's companies involved repeated and calculated collisions of tone and perspective which served to undermine any moral and philosophical positions adopted by the characters. Some of this satirical 'doubleness' of perspective survives in the tragicomedies of Fletcher and his collaborators but in a less jagged form, integrated more smoothly into the kind of elaborate plot with a 'surprise' happy ending which is characteristic of romance forms. Fletcher's famous definition of tragicomedy in his preface to *The Faithful Shepherdess* (1608) specifically focused on plot structure rather than tonal variety: 'A tragie-comedie is not so called in respect of mirth and killing, but in respect it wants deaths, which is inough to make it no tragedie, yet brings some neere it, which is inough to make it no comedie.'[3] Interacting interestingly first with Marston and then with Fletcher was, of course, Shakespeare, whose 'problem' comedies and late romances can all be classified as forms of tragicomedy, whether defined on the basis of tone or structure.

Seeing *The Devil's Law-Case* in relation to these other seventeenth-century experiments in tragicomedy can result in several different modern critical judgements. If Marston is seen as the dominant influence, then the satiric and intellectually challenging aspects of Webster's play will be emphasised and its close continuity with the tragedies, particularly *The White Devil*, will be more easy to assert. If Fletcher is taken as the reference point, then the complex plotting with its fortunate final twists will be highlighted and Webster will be convicted of sacrificing the artistic integrity of the tragedies for the sake of a fashionable but empty melodramatic formula which, moreover, he is incapable of imitating successfully. If the relation to Shakespeare is stressed, then the temptation will be to invest the miraculous happy ending with a religious and philosophical profundity of the kind that many critics have found in *Measure for Measure* or *The Winter's Tale*. Suggestive connections with other Jacobean plays can be multiplied almost endlessly though none of them definitively 'explains' the peculiarities of *The Devil's Law-Case* and comparisons with modern forms of dark comedy can be almost equally illuminating. Romelio's manically amoral plotting, such as his attempt to get his sister to feign pregnancy by the 'dead' Ercole, generates the kind of exchanges which are recognisably Ortonesque:

JOLENTA: How's this?
      Issue by him, he dead, and I a virgin?
ROMELIO: I knew you would wonder how it could be done. . .
                              (III. iii. 31–3)

This kind of 'indirect' critical approach to Webster's play, proceeding by a series of comparisons and contrasts, is probably more fruitful than a direct frontal assault on its characterisation and plotting. Even for admirers of Fletcher's style of melodrama, Webster has overloaded the narrative complications to the point of incoherence. The only near-contemporary comment on *The Devil's Law-Case* concedes (with implied approval) that 'the plot is intricate enough' before adding 'but if rightly scanned will be found faulty by reason many passages do either not hang together, or if they do it is so sillily that no man can perceive them likely to be ever done'.[4] Much of the motivation is obscure and self-contradictory in ways which can only partly be justified in terms of the kind of sustained exploration of moral ambiguity which Webster had conducted in *The White Devil*. There are indeed moments when the characters' edgy ethical uncertainty is brilliantly expressed. The warmth and closeness of Ercole's 'noble' embrace of Contarino before they fight their duel over Jolenta is interpreted as a suspicious frisk for concealed body armour: 'your jealousy gave that embrace to try / If I were arm'd, did it not?' (II. i. 301–2).[5] The fact that neither of these supposedly noble rivals ever comes properly into moral focus may well be intentional on Webster's part and we should not necessarily be puzzled over why, without explanation, Contarino breaks his vow not to fight a duel or Ercole chooses to lie about Romelio's furtherance of his suit to Jolenta. However, no amount of critical ingenuity will explain away Contarino's later decision not to reveal that he survived both the duel and Romelio's attempt to murder him, a decision which puts four lives pointlessly at risk (including his own). Webster foregrounds the problem by having Contarino exclaim, 'Wherefore should I with such an obstinacy, / Conceal myself any longer?' (V. ii. 18–19) but cannot provide a satisfactory answer. The nervous vitality and shifting tonalities of Webster's language help to compensate for many of the structural defects, but part of the problem is that much of the play's original appeal was grounded in the two aspects which are most elusive for modern readers: the topical and the theatrical – and it is these two aspects which I now wish to concentrate upon, before concluding with some remarks on the play's alleged moral and religious significance.

Although nominally set in Italy, like the two tragedies, *The Devil's Law-Case* contains a stream of references to such things as

the Gunpowder Plot, the New Exchange, and recent clashes between the Dutch and English in the East Indies. All of these help
to situate the play much more firmly in Jacobean London than
The White Devil or *The Duchess of Malfi* and so it is no surprise that
some of its subject matter seems to spring directly from topical
anxieties. One of these concerned the upsurge of duelling, which
had prompted James (who, having escaped a number of assassi-
nation attempts, had a personal horror of physical violence) to
issue several Proclamations in the years immediately preceding
The Devil's Law-Case. Webster's handling of this issue comes
across as characteristically ambivalent since his play is structured
round two very differently conceived duels. The first, despite its
veneer of gentlemanly honour, is subject to such condemnation
by church and state that any winner risks being judged a murderer and any loser denied burial as a suicide. The second,
despite its underlying absurdity (Contarino is one of the combat-
ants seeking to resolve the dispute over who killed him), is
staged with the full ritual authority of the state, involving a
Marshal, trumpets and formulaic language. As in many of the
period's revenge plays, the boundaries between socially sanc-
tioned forms of violence and criminal excesses are provocatively
explored.

Of equal or greater interest to many modern readers is the fact
that *The Devil's Law-Case* (whose full subtitle is *When Women Go
to Law the Devil is Full of Business*) seems to be a topically slanted
contribution to a perennial debate about the nature of women
and their role in society which flared up with particular force in
the years 1615–20, fuelled by a number of scandals and court
cases in which women were particularly prominent.[6] In 1618
Thomas Howard, Earl of Suffolk, was removed from the office of
Lord Treasurer, accused of corrupt practices which many thought
his wife had instigated. Both ended up in the Tower after a Star
Chamber hearing. Then in 1619 Sir Thomas Lake lost his position
as Secretary of State because of his wife's false and malicious allegations against the Countess of Exeter, allegations which were
disproved in another Star Chamber hearing. Again everyone
ended up in the Tower and some commentators were prepared
to sympathise with Lake because he was 'so over-awed by his
Wife, that if he did not what she commanded, she would beat
him, and in truth his Wife was afterward his over-throw'.[7] The

fact that Lady Lake's lying allegations were supported by per-
jured evidence from her maid increases the connection with
Webster's play and helps support the argument for a relatively
late dating. In any event, when writing a play about a litigious
woman, Webster would also have had in mind the long-running
dispute between Lady Hatton and Sir Edward Coke over his attempt to force their daughter into an advantageous political
marriage. The spectacle of the nation's former Chief Justice being
dragged through the courts by his own wife gave predictable
ammunition to those who thought that women were becoming
over-powerful, a body of opinion which included James himself.
Writing in February 1619, Chamberlain thought that 'the King is
in great vaine of taking downe highhanded women', and the following year Chamberlain records James's order to his clergy to
'inveigh vehemently and bitterly in theyre sermons against the
insolencie of our women'. Some of James's specific concern was
over inappropriately 'masculine' styles of dressing, an issue
which is not raised in *The Devil's Law-Case*, but the impression of
a general antifeminist backlash in which the theatre as well as the
clergy was involved is strengthened by another letter of Chamberlain's written shortly afterwards:

> Our pulpits ring continually of the insolence and impudence
> of women: and to helpe the matter forward the players have
> likewise taken them to taske, and so to the ballades and bal-
> lad-singers, so that they can come no where but theyre eares
> tingle: and yf all this will not serve the king threatens to fall
> upon theyre husbands, parents, or frends that have or shold
> have powre over them and make them pay for yt.[8]

Precisely where Webster's play fits into all this is not so clear.
Its full title, its trial scene in which a woman's malice is publicly
exposed, and a number of stray misogynist remarks by various
characters all seem to make it a plausible example of the way 'the
players have likewise taken [women] to taske'. An exchange between Crispiano and Ariosto at the beginning of Act III seems
particularly heavy with topical significance. We are told how the
King has been informed 'What mad tricks has been played of late
by ladies', how 'they use their lords as if they were their wards'
and call 'in question one another's honesties' (III. i. 9, 11, 21).

Crispiano concludes the scene by anticipating his judicial role in the trial:

> Well, I have vow'd
> That I will never sit upon the bench more,
> Unless it be to curb the insolencies
> Of these women.
>
> (III. i. 25–8)

Yet there are good reasons for thinking that *The Devil's Law-Case* pre-dates by at least a year the 1620 reference to the players taking women to task[9] and if the various allusions to forced marriages ('To be contracted / In tears, is but fashionable') are meant to recall the earlier Hatton–Coke quarrels then their effect is, if anything, to support Lady Hatton's view of the matter. The maid Winifred explicitly denounces such marriages as a social evil comparable to the bitterly opposed enclosures of common land:

> Force one to marry against their will! Why 'tis
> A more ungodly work than enclosing the commons.
>
> (I. ii. 191–2)

Indeed, Elizabethan and Jacobean plays frequently show a great deal of sympathy for women compelled to marry (or, in the case of the Duchess of Malfi, not to marry) against their will. They tend to resist co-option into the kind of antifeminist alliance referred to by Chamberlain. About the same time that *The Devil's Law-Case* was first performed by Queen Anne's Men, the same acting company was putting on *Swetnam, the Woman-hater, Arraigned by Women*, a lively comic response to *The Araignment of Lewde, Idle, Froward and Unconstant Women*, a misogynist pamphlet written in 1615 by Joseph Swetnam which had started a small pamphlet war. Webster's play should undoubtedly be situated within these contemporary arguments but it is difficult to see it as unequivocally lined up on one side or the other.

Its treatment of Leonora, the woman who launches the lawsuit which gives the play its title, is especially interesting. This elderly but still sexually active lady, who competes with her own daughter for Contarino's affections, could easily have been treated with a mixture of grotesquerie and pathos as a stock type whose most famous embodiment was to be Congreve's Lady Wishfort. Yet in her reaction to Contarino's apparent death, her great speech of grief and anger trembling on the brink of madness (III. iii. 238–82), she rises far beyond any misogynist stereotype. We are given another example of Webster's special talent for thrillingly suggesting the violent extremes of emotion to be found in the most unlikely characters. In what is so far the only modern revival of the play (directed by Michael Winter at the Theatre Royal, York, in 1980), some critics thought that the actress playing Leonora did not do enough to project this emotional violence: 'Leonora should be a sexy old woman of 60 but Annette Kerr hoses down the hot verse and turns the character into an up-market governess forced to handle soiled lines. She delivers them mildly with a cleansing smile which makes nonsense of motivation.'[10] In other words, the twentieth-century actress was accused of having a more 'decorous' conception of how old women should behave than the seventeenth-century dramatist. Moreover, the way in which the plot permits Leonora to 'win' the romantic contest with her daughter and walk off with Contarino at the end is itself a fascinating breach of both social and artistic expectations which complicates any contribution the play may have made to contemporary controversies about women.

The other particularly elusive aspect of *The Devil's Law-Case* for the modern reader (and in the absence of further modern productions it is only readers who will encounter the play) is its intense theatricality. In his Preface 'To the Judicious Reader' Webster wrote that 'A great part of the grace of this (I confess) lay in action' and reviewers of the Theatre Royal revival, despite differences of opinion, found much that was exciting in performance.[11] Like Webster's earlier plays, *The Devil's Law-Case* is extremely self-conscious about its theatrical status. The lawyer Contilupo says of the trial that it 'deserves / Rather a spacious public theatre / Than a pent court for audience' (IV. i. 102–4), a joke whose precise point would vary depending on whether the play was originally staged at the large, open-air, 'public' Red Bull or the smaller, indoor, 'private' Cockpit. Unfortunately, the printed text leaves many pieces of stage business obscure and only some of these have been satisfactorily clarified by modern editors. For instance, after we have seen Jolenta being forcibly kissed by Ercole she addresses Contarino, the man she really desires, with 'Hark in your ear, I'll show you his [Ercole's] right worthy / Demeanour to me' (I. ii. 227–8). D. C. Gunby's Penguin edition has no stage direction at this point, whilst Elizabeth Brennan's New Mermaids edition merely adds *'She whispers in his ear, and he embraces her'*. Yet the preceding business and the dialogue which follows suggest very strongly that she takes the initiative and kisses him in a 'forward' manner reminiscent of the Duchess's wooing of Antonio. This makes Jolenta a more interesting figure and gives an additional edge to Contarino's line 'If he bear himself so nobly. . .' (I. ii. 237).

It is in the area of costuming and disguise that a good deal of the play's performance value is to be found. Romelio's impersonation of a 'rare Italianated Jew' is not a very effective way of furthering his plots but has its own interest as a caricature of an existing theatrical caricature. Equipped with a large artificial nose and probably with the red hair and yellow gown traditionally worn by Judas, Romelio enters mouthing melodramatic villainies about betraying towns to the Turk and setting fire to the Christian navy, making it clear that his 'disguise' is primarily an opportunity to allude to and re-create Marlowe's villain-hero Barabas. The 1633 Quarto of *The Jew of Malta* speaks of it as having been played by 'her Majesties Servants at the *Cock-Pit*', with the part of Barabas being taken by Richard Perkins. The reference is almost certainly to the later Queen Henrietta's Men but it is quite possible that Perkins (who took the role of Flamineo in *The White Devil*) was already playing Barabas for Queen Anne's Men when Webster was writing *The Devil's Law-Case*. Perkins would have been the most likely casting for Romelio so Webster could have given him a splendid opportunity to parody his more famous role. This gives an additional self-referential force to the first lines spoken in the disguise:

> Excellently well habited! Why, methinks
> That I could play with mine own shadow now. . .
> (II. ii. 1–2)

Certainly, as far as Machiavellian efficiency is concerned, Romelio would have been better off remaining in his own shape. Contarino's surgeons do not trust him because 'He looks like a rogue' which is hardly surprising given his close resemblance to one of the theatre's most famous villains. Like Barabas himself, Romelio discovers that it is difficult to be a successful plotter whilst looking like a stage Machiavel. Rather than simply being a means to an end, it is the disguise itself which is the real object of interest, something which is confirmed by the way it eerily reappears at the end of the play, utilised by one of the surgeons whom it was originally intended to deceive.

In the great trial scene, no less than five of the onstage characters are in disguise, with two more (Leonora and her maid) having apparently altered their appearance significantly. It is typical of the difficulties presented by the printed text that only a stray remark several scenes later establishes that Contarino is meant to be in Danish costume. Nashe's caricature of 'The Pride of the Dane' in *Pierce Penniless* probably gives a better idea of how this was realised theatrically than any recollections of *Hamlet*. For Nashe, the stereotypical Dane was a mixture of braggart soldier and overdressed gallant:

> The most gross and senseless proud dolts. . . are the Danes, who stand so much upon their unwieldy burly-boned soldiery that they account of no man that hath not a battle-axe at his girdle to hough [hamstring] dogs with, or wears not a cock's feather in a red thrummed [tassled] hat like a cavalier. . . his apparel is so puffed up with bladders of taffety, and his back like beef stuffed with parsley, so drawn out with ribbons and devices, and blistered with light sarsenet [silken] bastings, that you would think him nothing but a swarm of butterflies if you saw him afar off.[12]

If Contarino's disguise *was* anything like this, then it must be connected satirically with the aristocratic pride which led him to fight the duel and with all the other instances of 'insolent vainglory' with which the play abounds. Oddly enough, in Act V Contarino is able to appear in the robes of a 'Bathanite' friar without sacrificing his Danish identity. The friar's costume may represent an ascetic critique of the 'vanity' of the Danish disguise but there has been no deep spiritual change in Contarino and no resumption, at this point, of 'real' identity. Similarly, Ercole's status as a Knight of Malta seems to offer more symbolic potential than Webster can coherently manipulate. In *The White Devil* he had effectively exploited the moral implications of a silver cross on a black background, but here it remains uncertain how much of the time Ercole appears in this regalia and to what effect. If he begins the play in this costume, then Jolenta's scepticism about 'men's outsides' (I. ii. 15) has immediate visual justification since she is being courted by a man whose garb signifies, among other things, a vow of chastity. Yet the suggestion of moral irony is not really sustained and Ercole comes to seem more and more worthy of Jolenta's hand. Like Contarino, he appears in friar's robes in Act V but whether these act as a similar critique of his earlier costuming and how they relate to his forthcoming success in winning Jolenta is impossible to say.

The Devil's Law-Case has many examples of Webster recycling moral emblems from his previous plays but confusing their significance by resituating them within the context of romantic melodrama. As well as a Knight of Malta, we have bellmen, a Capuchin, coffins, winding sheets and a Moorish disguise. These devices sometimes seem unmotivated and perfunctory, like Jolenta's appearance as a Moorish 'black' nun in order to form a tableau with Angiolella, the pregnant 'white' nun, and sometimes seem to border on self-parody. Confronted with the emblems of mortality which had brought the Duchess to her knees, Julio's reaction is jokingly to wrap the winding sheet round his neck in the form of a hangman's halter whilst Romelio feigns Christian penitence before locking his mother and the Capuchin in the closet. The general impression is of a wealth of theatrical symbolism, an excess of signification, which ultimately does not signify anything very much. The apparent gestures towards moral profundity seem too serious to be entirely parodic yet too perfunctory to be genuinely profound.

A number of critics have argued strongly for the essential seriousness of *The Devil's Law-Case*[13] and certainly there is both evidence of moral patterning and a sophisticated sense of moral ambiguity. We are repeatedly confronted with forms of arrogance and hubris which are repeatedly punished. Romelio sees the profit from his commercial enterprises as being 'as certain as the gain / In erecting a lottery' (I. i. 15–16). The unintended implications of the simile are fulfilled when his ships, all bearing confident names like 'The Storm's Defiance', are lost at sea.

Contarino seems to be winning the duel easily, having twice wounded Ercole, when he is 'lost in too much daring' and himself receives a near-fatal wound. More subtly, the Capuchin's attempt to 'play God', like the Duke in *Measure for Measure*, by witholding vital information as part of a stage-managed spiritual test, backfires disastrously. Yet Webster is also fascinated by the way that Romelio's arrogant refusal to be awed by the fate of the two duellists (they are to be treated as suicides and denied Christian burial) comes close to and is, at times, indistinguishable from a properly Christian sense of the irrelevance of earthly funeral arrangements:

> What care I then, though my last sleep,
> Be in the desert, or in the deep;
> No lamp, nor taper, day and night,
> To give my charnel chargeable light?
> I have there like quantity of ground,
> And at the last day I shall be found.
>   (II. iii. 126–31)

As in *The Duchess of Malfi*, there is a subtle probing of the fine distinction between spiritual confidence and the 'security' which 'some men call the suburbs of hell' (*DM*, V. iii. 334).

To point out the artificial, implausible and even absurd means by which *The Devil's Law-Case* reaches its happy ending is not automatically to reject its pretensions to moral and religious significance. Foregrounding the unlikely nature of a happy ending, as Shakespeare seems to do in *The Winter's Tale*, may be a deliberate strategy to evoke a sense of wonder which carries inescapable religious overtones. Protestant theology emphasised faith rather than reason as the path to God and writers were fond of quoting and elaborating upon Tertullian's famous rule of faith: 'Certum est quia impossibile est' [It is certain because it is impossible]. As far as Sir Thomas Browne was concerned, 'there be not impossibilities enough in Religion for an active faith'.[14] Calvinism, in particular, promoted the view that God's workings were secret and inscrutable, incapable of being understood or challenged by human reason. The darker consequences of this belief emerge clearly in the Capuchin's reflections on the gap between human intentions and their outcomes. A hidden and

predestinate sinfulness mysteriously subverts all attempts to act
rationally for the best:

> to see how heaven
> Can invert man's firmest purpose!
> . . . wretches turn
> The tide of their good fortune, and being drench'd
> In some presumptuous and hidden sins,
> While they aspire to do themselves most right,
> The devil that rules i'th' air, hangs in their light.
>
> (V. iv. 193–201)

A version of this last line had appeared in *The Duchess of Malfi* as
part of Antonio's view of Bosola as a man condemned to have
his best impulses cruelly frustrated. The more positive side of
this Calvinistic theology, which constituted the 'official' Anglicanism of Webster's period, was its corresponding emphasis on
the hidden and apparently 'irrational' workings of grace. It may
seem absurd that Romelio successfully resists the spiritual
pressure of the Capuchin, his mother and the emblems of
mortality, only to have a qualm of conscience a short while later.
One might cynically attribute this erratic behaviour to Webster's
unwillingness to forego the theatrical excitements of the ceremo-
nial combat (which is 'continued to a good length'). Yet the
'absurdity' of Romelio's change of heart belongs to a recog-
nisable tradition of Protestant theology which culminates in
Kierkegaard's 'leap of faith' and the Christian existentialism of
Karl Jaspers.

The decisive objection to taking *The Devil's Law-Case* as seriously as some critics have done is not its implausibility, which
can itself be a stimulus to profound speculation, but its lack of
emotional engagement at the end. We hardly care what happens
to the various characters and their expressions of joy seem perfunctory in the extreme (though arguably less so in performance,
where their words may be less important than their gestures).
The 'significance' of a tragedy is not simply the product of an interpretive strategy which invokes a philosophical or religious
context. It is rooted in the emotional response it is capable of
winning from an audience; and the same is true for certain forms
of tragicomedy which claim a comparable artistic importance.

The miraculous and 'absurd' conclusions of *Pericles* and *The Winter's Tale* are deeply moving. So, to take a more modern example, is the ending of Carl Dreyer's great film *The Word*, in which a young woman who has died in childbirth is brought back to life by a miracle of faith. Webster's unlikely ending has an altogether different and lesser effect. It is neither amusing enough to work as a parody of the desire for improbable happy endings nor emotional enough to seem deeply significant. Yet the play as a whole, even when more grandiose claims are rejected, remains lively, disconcerting, highly theatrical and much more interesting than many more 'competent' plays of the period. It remains, in other words, a suitable candidate for further revivals.

6
Ford and Caroline Theatre

John Ford was born in 1586, only eight years after Webster, but he did not begin writing for the theatre till he was approaching forty. Their careers overlapped briefly when they formed part of the team which produced the lost *A Late Murder of the Son upon the Mother* (1624). The previous year Ford had contributed an enthusiastic poem to the first Quarto of *The Duchess of Malfi* and they were probably both also involved in *The Fair Maid of the Inn* (1626), though Ford's contribution may have been limited to one scene (IV. i). Since Ford's major plays were not written till around 1630, he is normally represented in literary histories as belonging to a different theatrical generation from Webster and frequently spoken of as typifying some of the allegedly distinctive characteristics of Caroline drama. Despite recent successful revivals at the Swan of Shirley's *Hyde Park* (1632) and Brome's *A Jovial Crew* (1641), Ford remains by far the best known Caroline dramatist and *'Tis Pity She's a Whore* the one Caroline play frequently encountered in the modern theatre. However, the nature of theatrical activity in the reign of Charles has been subject to considerable scholarly re-evaluation and Ford's place within it looks more complicated than it did a generation ago.

Until recently, criticism of Caroline drama tended to be content with rehearsing a number of clichés about its decline from a Shakespearean high point. This decline, or 'decadence' (a term which conveniently combined moral and aesthetic implications), was seen as a consequence of the increased identification of the theatre with the court and the increased importance of the more exclusive indoor ('private') theatres. Both of these trends had begun under James, but Charles and his Queen, Henrietta Maria, took a much greater personal interest in the drama than James had ever done. Charles intervened directly in the censoring of play manuscripts and, on one occasion, provided a leading dramatist (Shirley) with the plot for *The Gamester*, declaring complacently afterwards that it was the best play he had seen for seven years. Henrietta, not content with the numerous court performances put on by the leading companies, visited the Blackfriars theatre on several occasions. She also acted in court plays, receiving coaching from Joseph Taylor, the principal actor of the King's Men. Under her influence the court became something of a theatre workshop with a number of courtiers being encouraged to try their hand at playwriting, the more successful productions transferring to the Blackfriars after being performed at court. All this helped to support a view that the fashionable indoor theatres were little more than an adjunct to a dominant court culture. The continued activity of the open-air public theatres was easy to ignore because much of it involved the revival of old-fashioned popular favourites like *Tamburlaine* rather than the writing of new plays. The artistic consequences of this received picture were alleged to be a narrower and politically enfeebled drama, appealing to a social élite rather than a nation, and incapable of biting the courtly hand which fed it.

The appearance in the 1970s of a complete annotated edition of Massinger's plays, followed in the 1980s by some important scholarly and critical books, has made it easier to give a more accurate and complex account of Caroline theatre than the one which appears in older works like Harbage's *Cavalier Drama*.[1] Although the court helped to foster certain forms of dramatic activity, such as the pastoral plays which Henrietta herself appeared in, it was neither aesthetically nor politically monolithic and remained open to plays which were critical of royal policy such as Habington's *The Queen of Aragon* (1640). Moreover, court drama represented only a small fraction of the total theatrical activity in London which, despite the fact that the King's Men staged a number of plays by courtly amateurs, remained a predominantly commercial and professional operation with its own traditions. The social gap between the private and public theatres undoubtedly increased but continued to exhibit some of the complexities mentioned in chapter 2, with both plays and companies moving at times between the different kinds of venue. Ford himself worked mainly, but not exclusively, for the indoor 'private' theatres.

The most obvious breach of continuity which occurred in 1625 was not the result of a new monarch being crowned but of the terrible plague which raged in London that year. In an eerie repeat of the events of 1603, the accession of the new king was accompanied by one of the worst outbreaks of pestilence since the Black Death in the fourteenth century. By the end of the year plague deaths in London had exceeded 35,000, and among the victims was John Fletcher, leading writer for the King's Men and the man who had done more than anyone to shape the direction of later Jacobean drama. The theatres, which had been closed in mourning for James from 27 March, were not permitted to reopen until the end of November. The effect of this enforced commercial break was to bankrupt every existing company apart from the King's Men. The death of Middleton two years later seemed to confirm the end of a theatrical era.

Yet when playing resumed in late 1625, the pattern of theatrical activity in London was essentially the same as it had been since 1616. Dominating the scene were the King's Men, now with Massinger as their main playwright, performing at the indoor Blackfriars in winter and the outdoor Globe in summer. The enduring pre-eminence of this company, rooted in sound financial arrangements, continuity of personnel and the marvellous stock of plays in their repertoire, was the most important source of theatrical stability between 1603 and 1642. From 1625 until 1636, when another severe outbreak of plague caused further theatrical bankruptcies, their main rivals were Queen Henrietta's Men, playing at the Cockpit (or Phoenix) theatre and employing Shirley as their resident dramatist. During the last years of James's reign, Christopher Beeston had moved a number of companies in and out of the Cockpit but it was only under Charles that his theatre came to equal the Blackfriars in social esteem. All Ford's major plays were written for one or other of these two playhouses. In 1629 a third indoor theatre, the Salisbury Court, was

erected, but it did not succeed in breaking the fashionable
duopoly established by the Blackfriars and the Cockpit. Meanwhile, the large open-air public theatres, the Red Bull and the
Fortune, continued to play to 'Citizens, and the meaner sort of
people', relying mainly on the kind of spectacular 'drum and
trumpet' plays which had maintained their popular appeal since
the 1590s.

The evidence for two distinct dramatic 'traditions' based on
the two different types of playhouse and appealing to two different audiences is quite strong but remains an over-simplification.
The Cockpit retained in its repertoire many plays that had first
been performed at the Red Bull, which was why, in the theatrical
quarrel which broke out in 1630, the courtier poet Carew was
able to sneer at 'that adulterate stage' (the Cockpit).[2] The companies which played at the new Salisbury Court indoor theatre
in the 1630s also performed, apparently without problems, at the
Red Bull and the Fortune. Most importantly, the King's Men continued to play at both kinds of theatre up to 1642. Undoubtedly
they moved some of their repertoire back and forth between the
Blackfriars and the Globe but there is a lack of hard evidence
about which plays, if any, were thought unsuitable for transfer.
Ford's two surviving Blackfriars plays, *The Lover's Melancholy*
and *The Broken Heart*, do not look likely candidates for performance in a large open-air venue but the first of them *was* actually
staged at the Globe during the summer months and we have no
evidence that the second was not also. The argument put forward in chapter 2 that the differences between Jacobean theatres
were more social than aesthetic is less true of the Caroline period
but still has some force. Rather than conceive of two wholly
distinct audiences for plays, it is more accurate to think in terms
of overlapping groups, with the Globe continuing to perform a
mediating role. The audiences for plays at court would then form
a third, much smaller, subset, genuinely exclusive in a way that
no commercial theatre audience could be.

The special characteristics of Caroline plays, including their
supposed 'decadence', owe more to their necessarily anxious relationship with the mass of already existing drama than to
changes in the social composition of their audiences. Moreover,
any generalisations about Caroline taste which base themselves
entirely on new plays are seriously misleading. Although the

King's Men performed about four new works each year, their repertory was dominated by the proven successes of the previous forty years, particularly the plays of Fletcher, Shakespeare and Jonson. Of the twenty-one plays the King's Men put on at court in 1630–1, only a couple (including Ford's lost *Beauty in a Trance*) were new. Most of the others were between ten and thirty-five years old. It is hard to deplore as 'decadent' the taste of a court still keen to watch *A Midsummer Night's Dream* (*c*.1595), *Volpone* (1606) or *The Maid's Tragedy* (*c*.1610) and in this respect the court's preferences were the same as those of the commercial theatre audiences. Complimentary verses attached to Massinger's *The Roman Actor* (printed in 1629) complain that 'of late, 'tis true / The old accepted are more then the new'.[3] In most phases of theatre history, changes of taste render the previous generation's work 'stale' to succeeding audiences, thus clearing the ground for new writers and new forms of dramaturgy to emerge. Ford, however, faced a situation in which his immediate predecessors had become established classics without any intervening loss of popularity. He was forced to compete for an audience with the giants of the recent past who seemed, with their vast theatrical output, to have used up every possible plot, type of character or style of writing, and to have done so in ways which could not be improved upon but only weakly echoed. Dryden, writing after the Restoration, was to make this point with particular force:

> not only shall we never equal them [the dramatists of the previous age], but they could never equal themselves, were they to rise and write again. We acknowledge them our fathers in wit, but they have ruined their estates themselves before they came to their children's hands. There is scarce an humour, a character, or any kind of plot, which they have not used. All comes sullied or wasted to us.[4]

Ford's early plays represent a number of characters as crushed by the burden of the past, unable to develop fully in consequence, and it is hard not to see their plight as a displaced version of his own fears. His Prologue to his first published play, *The Lover's Melancholy*, contains anxious assertions of originality:

> Our writer, for himself, would have ye know
> That in his following scenes he doth not owe
> To others' fancies; nor hath lain in wait
> For any stolen invention from whose height
> He might commend his own, more than the right
> A scholar claims may warrant for delight.

There is a similar claim in the Prologue to his late tragicomedy, *The Fancies Chaste and Noble*, where he insists that 'in it is shown / Nothing but what our author knows his own / Without a learned theft'.

Ford might protest as much as he likes but critics have continued to view his work as a self-conscious set of variations on situations and characters already familiar to his audience. *Love's Sacrifice* complicates *Othello* by replaying it with a less obviously innocent Desdemona. *'Tis Pity* gives a new edge to *Romeo and Juliet* by combining the tragic tale of two young lovers with a Faustus-like challenge to the existing moral order. The crucial critical act consists not in recognising these allusions and reworkings, since many of them are unmissable, but in deciding what sort of effect Ford was aiming at. Martin Butler has argued that Ford's work springs from the same Inns of Court culture which had earlier generated Marston's plays.[5] In other words, Ford is conceived of as primarily addressing a circle of highly knowledgeable and experienced theatre-goers, many of them with their own literary ambitions. His many theatrical 'quotations' would, in Butler's view, be forms of self-consciously witty display designed to elicit knowing recognition and appealing to a shared connoisseurship. What is missing from this otherwise plausible account is an acknowledgement of the particular problems of the tragic writer who needs to make an audience *feel* rather than simply feel clever. Ford's self-conscious reworkings of previous plays are part of a continuing struggle to achieve authentic emotional expression despite the suffocating pressure of the 'already written'. It is to this end that he complicates the situations and simplifies the language of his predecessors. His irony and allusiveness are not ends in themselves but necessary strategies for the communication of feelings to an audience which has lost its artistic 'innocence'. Shakespeare's plays must have seemed powerfully 'modern' and emotionally realistic in comparison with previous Tudor drama, but the moment always comes when the 'modern' in art can go no further, having apparently exhausted the expressive possibilities of a particular form. This would leave a writer like Ford, who still wished to move his audiences, with a difficult and characteristically 'postmodern' problem which he solved in the postmodern manner described by Umberto Eco:

> The postmodern reply to the modern consists of recognizing that the past, since it cannot really be destroyed, because its destruction leads to silence, must be revisited: but with irony, not innocently. I think of the postmodern attitude as that of a man who loves a very cultivated woman and knows he cannot say to her, 'I love you madly,' because he knows that she knows (and that she knows that he knows) that these words have already been written by Barbara Cartland. Still, there is a solution. He can say, 'As Barbara Cartland would put it, I love you madly.' At this point, having avoided false innocence, having said clearly that it is no longer possible to speak innocently, he will nevertheless have said what he wanted to say to the woman: that he loves her, but he loves her in an age of lost innocence. If the woman goes along with this, she will have received a declaration of love all the same. Neither of the two speakers will feel innocent, both will have accepted the challenge of the past, of the already said, which cannot be eliminated; both will consciously and with pleasure play the game of irony. . . . But both will have succeeded, once again, in speaking of love.[6]

Ford may have played the game of irony with his knowledgeable audience but the justification of the game was that he succeeded, once again, in speaking of love, grief, hatred, jealousy and all the other human emotions exhaustively dramatised by his predecessors. He confronted and overcame the particular problems facing a tragic writer in the Caroline period though these, it could be argued, were not dissimilar to the problems facing all writers, whatever their period, who attempt emotional realism despite the deadening weight of the 'already said'. The extremism and literary self-consciousness of *'Tis Pity She's a Whore* (c.1630), the way it needs both to acknowledge and go beyond previous plays in order to move its audience, is often seen as typifying Caroline 'decadence', but is it so very different from the extremism and literary self-consciousness of *Titus Andronicus* (c.1590), which mingles rape, mutilation and cannibalism with allusions to Ovid and Seneca in a manner that is both shocking and knowing? All writers of tragedy must engage with and surpass their predecessors in order to achieve the desired emotional effects. Ford's case is special only in that he had more to surpass than most dramatists since his predecessors continued to hold the stage as if they were his immediate contemporaries rather than revered but distant classics. Most dramatists would find direct competition with Shakespeare a problem.

Ford was the second son of a substantial Devonshire landowner and thus entitled, unlike Webster, to call himself a gentleman. He may have briefly been at Exeter College, Oxford, before, like Marston and possibly Webster too, he became a member of the Inns of Court, being admitted to the Middle Temple in 1602. To be a law student in London at that time was to be exposed, with all the shock and delight of the new, to some of the most powerful plays ever written. A number of details in Ford's early prose works suggest that he was a keen theatre-goer from very early on and was to carry with him permanently the mark of these first encounters. Although he never seems to have become a lawyer, he remained at the Middle Temple for many years, perhaps for most of his life. It was not necessary to be either a student or practitioner of law to remain in residence at the Inns of Court. Gentlemen with literary interests continued to be welcome, as long as they paid their bills (which Ford failed to do at one point, resulting in a two-year suspension from 1606 to 1608).

He probably did not begin writing for the theatre until 1621[7] but, prior to then, he published a number of other works which are interesting for the light they throw on the plays. The first of these was *Fames Memoriall* (1606), a poetic tribute to the recently deceased Earl of Devonshire, Lord Mountjoy. Ford dedicated his poem to Mountjoy's widow, Lady Penelope, the 'Stella' of Sidney's famous sonnet sequence and sister to the ill-fated Earl of Essex. In 1581 she had been forced into an arranged marriage with Lord Rich. Defying convention, she carried on an open affair with her real love, Mountjoy, bearing him five children. Ironically, she seems to have attracted serious social disapproval only when she tried to regularise her position by gaining a divorce from Rich in late 1605 and promptly marrying Mountjoy. His death three months later was seen by some as precipitated by the condemnation this marriage attracted. It is not hard to see in this story of forced marriage, enduring emotional loyalty and defiance of a hypocritically flexible social morality some of the preoccupations which drive Ford's plays. In his art, however, these conflicts of values appear absolute and hence tragic, whereas in life they seemed to have been resolved a good deal more pragmatically.

In another and briefer eulogy to Mountjoy, Ford wrote that the worst his enemies could allege against the Earl was that 'Dev'nshire did love'.[8] Ford chooses to see this as a mark of heroic virtue ('and did not Hercules / Feele beauties flame') rather than a moral blemish. His other major publication of 1606, *Honor Triumphant*, also apparently commits itself to the defence of chivalric attitudes to love. Written in connection with the jousts and tournaments which accompanied the visit to England of James's brother-in-law Christian IV of Denmark, *Honor Triumphant* represents four Earls offering to maintain by force of arms the following propositions: (i) 'Knights in Ladies service have no free will', (ii) 'Beauty is the mainteiner of valour', (iii) 'Faire Ladie was never false' and (iv) 'Perfect lovers are onely wise'. There has been considerable disagreement about Ford's tone of voice in this work and hence its relationship to his treatment of love in the plays. The prevailing manner is one of detached and witty artifice but courtly poses are often capable of accommodating a degree of irony without wholly deconstructing themselves. The helplessness which many of Ford's characters feel in the face of romantic desires is here given its most positive interpretation and some of Giovanni's Neoplatonic arguments are prefigured. However, no single work of Ford's is capable of yielding the master-code which will unlock the significance of his major plays. At the very least, the courtly attitudes of *Honor Triumphant* need to be set against the Christian and Stoic positions of his other non-dramatic works in order to understand the conflicts which structure the plays.

A radically different side to Ford's sensibility appears in *Christes Bloodie Sweat*, a long religious poem meditating on the sufferings of Jesus and, in particular, the agony in the garden when, according to St Luke, 'his sweat was as it were great drops of blood falling down to the ground'. Published in 1613 as by 'I. F.', it is now generally accepted as Ford's work, partly because of close verbal parallels with passages from his plays. In general terms, the poem is a strong reminder of how far the vivid representation of emotional and physical suffering in Elizabethan and Stuart tragedy is rooted in specifically Christian structures and habits of feeling. When Ford, out of earnest Protestant piety, attempts to make a firm distinction between passion and playing, he only succeeds in strengthening the resemblance:

> He di'd indeed not as an actor dies
> To die to day, and live againe to morrow,
> In shew to please the audience, or disguise
> The idle habit of inforced sorrow:
>   The Crosse his stage was, and he plaid the part
>   Of one that for his friend did pawne his heart.
> (ll. 889–94)

Dying in order to rise again another day is precisely what Christ does do, of course, and the figures of speech in the final couplet, including the apparent allusion to *The Merchant of Venice*, re-create the parallel which is being rejected. Some of the Friar's arguments in *'Tis Pity* can be traced back to this poem, just as some of Giovanni's counter-arguments have their source in *Honor Triumphant*, but scenes of tragic suffering, and the pity which they impel, need not be accompanied by a Christian moral position to be seen as the products of a Christian sensibility, accustomed to meditating on 'the Sonne of God in His Agonie'.

In the same year that *Christes Bloodie Sweat* appeared, Ford published another anonymous work whose authorship was only firmly established in the twentieth century. This was *The Golden Meane*, a work of humanist moral philosophy *'Discoursing* The Noblenesse of perfect Vertue in extreames' and drawing heavily on Seneca and other Stoics. A second edition the following year carried a daring acknowledgement of its previously concealed dedicatee, the Earl of Northumberland, who had been impris-

oned in the Tower since 1605 for his alleged involvement in the
Gunpowder Plot and whom Ford clearly believed to be innocent.
In 1620 Ford produced a similar philosophical work, *A Line of
Life*, this time dedicated to Northumberland's son-in-law, Sir
James Hay. These two pamphlets, with their classical emphasis
on 'resolution' as the prime moral virtue, constitute a third form
of discourse, neither Christian nor chivalric, though capable of
being partially assimilated into either mode. Their relation to the
drama is particularly strong since 'The Noblenesse of perfect Vertue in extreames' would be an apt subtitle for several of Ford's
plays, the celebration of an inward constancy being particularly
marked in *The Broken Heart, Perkin Warbeck, The Queen* and *The
Lady's Trial*.

It is apparent that in these non-dramatic works Ford exploited
a number of available discourses in ways which amounted to
more than a set of rhetorical exercises and less than a defining
personal philosophy. Within the confines of each work, his
imaginative engagement with the chosen rhetoric gave it an absolute and unquestioned character, something which does not
survive scrutiny of the different positions taken in different
works. The satisfying complexity of the plays derives from the
way they recombine *all* the discursive possibilities of the earlier
work into patterns of tension and opposition. The Friar in *'Tis
Pity* speaks as eloquently in his own way as Giovanni does in his.
If both seem at times to speak with Ford's voice, it is because
Ford had more than one voice.

Like Webster twenty years before, Ford began writing plays in
partnership with the indefatigable Dekker, getting the best possible apprenticeship in how to craft a saleable product. Between
1621 and 1624 he worked with Dekker, either as co-author or as
part of a team, on at least seven plays for a number of different
companies and theatres. They were *The Witch of Edmonton* (1621),
The Spanish Gypsy (1623), *The Welsh Ambassador* (1623), *The Sun's
Darling, The Fairy Knight, A Late Murder of the Son upon the Mother*
and *The Bristow Merchant* (all 1624). The last three titles are lost
and those which survive are sufficiently varied and sufficiently
different from Ford's later plays to suggest a competent professional at work rather than an 'auteur' of distinctive genius. *The
Witch of Edmonton*, a domestic tragedy (with Rowley as third
author) which deals with bigamy, witchcraft and murder, was

originally produced for Prince Charles's Men at the Cockpit but was successful enough to be revived for court performance, and it remains the only play of Ford's, apart from *'Tis Pity*, to have been produced professionally more than twice in the twentieth century. It has many obvious virtues – the ease and naturalness of much of the dialogue, the quirky humour of the devil-dog's relationship with the clown Cuddy, and the realism with which the small rural community is presented (something particularly emphasised in Barry Kyle's 1981 production for the RSC) – but these strengths probably derive mostly from Dekker and Rowley. Ford is usually seen as responsible for the Frank Thorney episodes and it is only in these that we find the recognisably Fordian combination of an inescapable fate met with quiet nobility. As he slips further into sin, Frank exclaims 'In vain he flees whose destiny pursues him' (II. i. 228) but by the time he goes repentant to the scaffold he is able to declare calmly 'He is not lost, / Who bears his peace within him' (V. iii. 73–4).

Ford only contributed a couple of scenes to *The Welsh Ambassador* but is normally credited with a larger share in the tragicomedy *The Spanish Gypsy* (despite a 1653 title page attribution to Middleton and Rowley) and the 'moral masque' *The Sun's Darling*. Both plays seem to glance at the foreign policy crisis of the early 1620s when James's reluctance to support his Protestant son-in-law Frederick of Bohemia in the Thirty Years' War and his pursuit of a Spanish marriage for Charles infuriated many of his subjects. *The Sun's Darling*, in particular, with its unmistakable allusions to the Winter King and Queen (as Frederick and Elizabeth were called, following their brief occupancy of the Bohemian throne), has been seen as endorsing the militant Protestant line consistently favoured by Dekker.[9] The fact that both plays were staged by the Lady Elizabeth's Men increases the likelihood that they carried coded comments on the policies which had left James's daughter, the company's patron, an impoverished exile in the Netherlands.

As well as the known collaborations with Dekker, Ford may have engaged in other joint projects during this phase of his career. As already mentioned, one scene of *The Fair Maid of the Inn* is probably his, since it carries the linguistic markers ('d'ee' and 't'ee' used for 'd'ye' and 't'ye') which have proved most reliable in distinguishing Ford's hand. The arguments for his part, or even sole, authorship of another 'Beaumont and Fletcher' play, *The Laws of Candy* (*c*.1621), are much weaker, despite the confident ascription of the entire work to him in the current edition of one of the standard scholarly reference works.[10] Whatever further plays Ford may or may not have had a hand in, this period of theatrical apprenticeship was largely over by the end of 1624 and was succeeded by a pause of about four years.

As in the case of Webster, it is difficult to reconcile the competent toiler in Dekker's workshop with the proud and self-conscious literary artist who emerges some years later. In the published text of what was probably his first independent play, *The Lover's Melancholy* (licensed for performance in November 1628 and printed in 1629), Ford presents himself as a gentleman-amateur writing for other gentlemen rather than as a professional catering to popular tastes. In the Epistle Dedicatory, addressed to friends at the Inns of Court, he writes, 'As plurality hath reference to a multitude, so I care not to please many' (a sentiment familiar from the works of Chapman, Jonson and Webster), while the Prologue dissociates Ford still further from the vulgarities of commercial endeavour:

> It is arts' scorn that some of late have made
> The noble use of poetry a trade.

The Epilogue goes on to imply that the author does not need to write for a living and will therefore not trouble his audience with a second play, if this one should prove unpleasing. The obvious incongruity of these sentiments with Ford's activities a few years earlier raises the whole problem of Ford's financial circumstances and the degree to which he *was* dependent on the stage for his livelihood. Although from a higher social background than Webster, Ford may at times have been more desperately in need of money than the prosperous coachmaker's son. His temporary suspension from the Middle Temple from 1606 to 1608 for non-payment of bills has already been mentioned and when his father died in 1610, he was left only £10. In the manuscript version of *A Line of Life*, written just before he began to work with Dekker, he speaks in the Dedication of 'the povertye of my uncomforted studies' and of being 'farr beneath the happynes of thriving fortunes', before signing himself with an aristocratic flourish 'John de la Ford'. By the time he came to write *The Lover's Melancholy*, his financial situation seems to have improved, perhaps through his obtaining some kind of legal work, and he was able to re-emphasise his 'amateur' status.

The Lover's Melancholy, written for the King's Men and performed at both the Blackfriars and the Globe, is a tragicomedy which owes an explicit debt to the analysis of mental disease in Burton's *Anatomy of Melancholy* and a more generally implicit one to Shakespeare's late romances. The acknowledged dependence on Burton in this play was to become the basis of G. F. Sensabaugh's famous argument that Ford's 'modernity' consisted partly in his acceptance of a 'scientific' and determinist view of human nature, divorced from ethical or religious perspectives.[11] Among the many defects of Sensabaugh's thesis was its over-emphasis on the 'typicality' of *The Lover's Melancholy* within the Ford canon and the consequent marginalisation of *Perkin Warbeck*, a rather better play. Nevertheless, *The Lover's Melancholy*, together with *The Broken Heart*, continues to be regarded as one of Ford's most characteristic plays, perhaps because here he succeeded for the first time in finding a rhythm, a tone of voice, a simplicity of phrasing, which stands out clearly from previous Elizabethan and Jacobean dramatic rhetoric:

> Parthenophill is lost and I would see him,
> For he is like to something I remember
> A great while since, a long, long time ago.
> (IV. iii. 28–30)

In this story of two men restored to happiness by the return of a lost woman, Ford was not carrying out a 'scientific' examination of human nature so much as struggling to restore some of the emotional power of Shakespeare's last plays which had been lost in Fletcherian tragicomedy. He did this by shifting the emphasis away from formulaic plot twists and onto the inner mental states of the characters, which were conveyed in a language simple enough to seem fresh even when it echoed Shakespeare ('Great, gracious sir, alas, why do you mock me? / I am a weak old man . . .').

The limited but real achievement of *The Lover's Melancholy* becomes more apparent if one compares it with another tragicomedy, *The Queen*, printed anonymously in 1653 and only attributed to Ford in the twentieth century. No one has succeeded in dating this play with any certainty but it may be among Ford's earliest independent works. By means of some preposterous plotting, a number of oppositions between love, honour and duty are established and exploited in the worst Fletcherian manner. In this play, the theatrical coup of an execution prevented at the last moment appealed to Ford so much that he attempted it three times, rather diminishing its shock value. Some of Ford's preoccupations, such as the deep importance attached to vows, are given extensive treatment but in a mechanical and external way which does not succeed in transforming the stale generic formula.

The auspices of *The Queen* remain unknown, but after *The Lover's Melancholy* Ford wrote two further plays for the King's Men, the lost *Beauty in a Trance* (performed at court on 28 November 1630) and *The Broken Heart*, all his other plays being written for companies at the Cockpit theatre. The precise order and dates of Ford's major plays are uncertain but the most plausible hypothesis, supported by authorities like G. E. Bentley and Andrew Gurr, is that around 1630, at the height of his powers, Ford left the King's Men and began writing for their main rivals, Queen Henrietta's Men. A likely sequence would then be *The Broken Heart* (1629), *'Tis Pity She's a Whore* (1630), *Love's Sacrifice* (1631) and *Perkin Warbeck* (1632). Ford's change of company was probably a consequence of the quarrel which began in 1630 between the new courtier-dramatists like Davenant, some of whose work was now being staged at the Blackfriars, and fully professional playwrights like Shirley and Massinger.[12] The courtiers favoured a more extravagant style of dramatic poetry and succeeded in at least temporarily imposing their taste at the Blackfriars, causing a couple of plays by Massinger, still the leading dramatist of the King's Men, to be poorly received. Despite sharing some friends with Davenant and despite his gentleman-amateur poses, Ford's theatrical apprenticeship had been thoroughly professional and he tended to avoid unnecessary stylistic complexity. At that particular moment in 1630, the Cockpit (for which many of the Dekker collaborations had been written) must have seemed more closely in touch with the professional playwriting traditions he was familiar with, whilst still rivalling the Blackfriars as a fashionable venue.

There does seem to be a small but distinctive shift in style between Ford's Blackfriars plays and his renewed work for the Cockpit. *The Lover's Melancholy* and *The Broken Heart* seem at times closer to pieces of rarefied mood music than representations of 'men in action', whereas the Cockpit tragedies are much more conventionally dramatic. *'Tis Pity* achieves a ferocious intensity unique in Caroline theatre, prompting occasional suggestions that it should be dated much earlier and seen as a Jacobean tragedy. *Perkin Warbeck* likewise seems to re-create an older dramatic form, in this case the Elizabethan history play. The Prologue begins by admitting that 'Studies have of this nature been of late / So out of fashion, so unfollowed' and its unshowy, solidly crafted virtues, resembling those of Massinger's best plays, would hardly have appealed much to the courtier poets installed at the Blackfriars. They would have found more to admire in *Love's Sacrifice*, with its presentation of a Platonic courtship so passionate that it only technically fails to be classifiable as adulterous. For the modern reader, this is Ford's least satisfactory tragedy and the only one which still awaits a professional revival. More than many Stuart plays subject to similar criticisms, the power of *Love's Sacrifice* can be felt in particular scenes rather than in its overall design. A modern production would be worth seeing simply for the scene (V. i) in which the Duke interrupts Bianca with her lover and savagely abuses her, only to have her respond with a superb and wounding arrogance of her own. The fact that Bianca is neither wholly guilty nor wholly innocent tempers the emotional violence with a strange objectivity and increases its resemblance to the great Soranzo–Annabella scene in *'Tis Pity She's a Whore*.

Ford completed his career with two undistinguished tragicomedies, both turning on the theme of virtue brought wrongfully into suspicion. *The Fancies Chaste and Noble* (c.1635) was the last play he wrote for Queen Henrietta's Men before they were bankrupted by the plague of 1636–7. When the theatres reopened, Beeston installed a new troupe in the Cockpit, the King and Queen's Young Company (otherwise known as Beeston's Boys). Ford wrote his last play for them, *The Lady's Trial* (licensed for performance in 1638), before perhaps retiring to his native Devonshire and disappearing from surviving records. It is not known when he died.

Ford has often been represented as endorsing a distinctively aristocratic code of values. According to Clifford Leech, 'his view of society was intensely class-conscious, and his ideal human being, though far removed from any conceivable norm, was in essence a courtier who would win King Charles's praise'.[13] This aristocratic outlook was seen as a corollary of his status as a coterie dramatist, writing for a small but sophisticated circle of courtiers and gentry: 'Shakespeare had written for all men . . . but Ford wrote for men and women who might dream of dying with the upper-class dignity of Ithocles and Calantha.'[14] The truth is rather more complicated than this since Ford was closer to the traditions of popular theatre than Leech allows, and 'aristocratic' values were not confined to the upper-classes in Renaissance England. The Protestant martyrs celebrated by Foxe faced death with a courage and dignity which might conform to an aristocratic ideal but which had no connection with actual social class. Ford's own treatment of the low-born Perkin Warbeck is enough to establish that for him, as for D. H. Lawrence, aristocracy was a spiritual rather than a social matter.

The values which mattered to Ford were also important to Shakespeare, and it is worth reflecting whether there really was such a large ideological gap between the two dramatists. Both, for instance, use comic counterpointing to qualify, without cancelling, the nobler sentiments expressed by their aristocratic protagonists. Ford, however, seems to have been somewhat schizophrenic about the value of low comedy in serious plays, making considerable use of it at times but also denouncing it in the Prologues to *The Broken Heart* and *Perkin Warbeck* ('nor is here / Unnecessary mirth forced, to endear / A multitude'). This ambivalence typifies the fact that, like Webster, Ford was a product of the interplay of different theatrical traditions. He thought of his major plays as serious works of literature addressed to an audience of like-minded gentlemen but he had also learnt with Dekker how to satisfy more popular tastes, being involved in at least one Red Bull play and probably others. It should be remembered that *The Lover's Melancholy*, despite the coterie nature of its Dedication to Inns of Court friends, was staged at the Globe as well as the Blackfriars. Moreover, Ford's unfashionable enthusiasm for tragedy, like his move back to the 'adulterate' Cockpit and his revival of the history play, could be seen as a sign of commitment to the popular Shakespearean tradition as well as a symptom of high literary ambition, which it undoubtedly also was.

Ford's political and religious views are not easily deducible from his works. The possible topical significance of *Perkin Warbeck* will be discussed in chapter 9 but, in general, his plays do not seem to engage directly with the controversial events of the 1630s, when Charles attempted to rule without Parliament and Laud challenged the Calvinist Protestant consensus by re-emphasising the importance of ritual and questioning the doctrine of predestination. If *The Queen* is a later play than I have suggested, then one might be able to see the wilful and tyrannical behaviour of Alphonso the King as a comment on Charles's personal rule. Especially significant would be the manner in which, at the end of the play, Alphonso voluntarily curbs his absolutist tendencies: 'henceforth beleeve me, / I'll strive to be a servant to the State' (V. 3702–4). However, this is a relatively minor and disputable example and it is significant that the two main books which examine drama and politics in the period immediately before the civil war hardly mention Ford.[15] The simplest explanation would be that Ford's main plays were written just before the real period of crisis, but there is a more important general point to be made. The Prologue to *The Lady's Trial* comments sarcastically on the kinds of playwright who are now considered fashionable and from whom Ford wishes to distance himself. These include the sort 'who idly scan affairs of state'. This is a late reminder (the play was printed in 1639) of the fact that Ford's approach to life, including recent historical events, had never been primarily political. He was more interested in tracing the disturbances and conflicts of the human heart than in commenting on contemporary politics.

In the non-dramatic works, the fates of various great men are presented in moral and tragic terms, rather than from a particular political perspective. In *The Golden Meane* the Earl of Essex is described pityingly as being 'cast downe by envie' (122), but his inveterate enemy Robert Cecil is later praised for the way the excellence of his mind overcame his physical defects (516–20). Similarly, the Dedications of his various works, despite some intriguing examples such as the one to the imprisoned Northumberland, do not form the kind of pattern which would associate Ford with a particular political faction in the way that Massinger's connections with the Herberts link him to a strongly Protestant aristocratic opposition to Charles's policies.[16] An early play like *The Sun's Darling*, which *does* seem to 'idly scan affairs of state', probably reflects Dekker's priorities rather than Ford's since its militant Protestant undercurrent does not fit very well with Ford's recent praise of James in *A Line of Life* as 'A Good man, that even with his entrance to the Crowne, did not more bring *peace* to all Christian nations, yea almost to all Nations of the Westerne World, then since the whole course of his glorious reigne, hath preserved [that] *peace* amongst them' (785–9). Even allowing for conventions of flattery, this does not read like the opinion of a man who thought James should do more to combat the forces of European Catholicism.

Judging from *Christes Bloodie Sweat*, Ford's religious views were probably typical of moderate English Protestants. There are a number of specific references to Calvinist doctrine but these tend to be subsumed into more general reflections on the saving power of Christ's suffering. The most strongly Calvinist stanza of the entire poem moderates into something more comfortingly redemptive in its last few lines:

> Yet neither did the *Death* or *Bloodie sweat*
> Of *Christ*, extend to soules ordain'd to Hell:
> But to the chosen, and elect, beget
> A double life, although the Scriptures tell
> How this meeke *Lambe of God* did chiefly come
> To call the lost sheepe, and the strayers home.
>
> (1687–93)

The devotional form of the poem is in fact more typical of Catholic than Protestant religious literature and, later on, Ford is able to speak approvingly of parents telling their children that Christ died so 'That every one might be redeem'd from hell' (1800), without apparently being aware of any contradiction.

We do not know what Ford thought of Laud's controversial reforms but there is something in his plays, particularly *The Broken Heart*, which is peculiarly homologous with the Laudian stress on the value of ritual. Critics of Laud, such as the puritan William Prynne, routinely damned ritualism, Catholicism and the theatre by a process of mutual association: 'The Popish Masse is now no other but a *Tragicke Play*. . . . Loe here, a Roman Masse-priest becomes a *Player*, and in stead of preaching, of reading, acts Christs Passion in the Masse.'[17] Ford himself may have consciously rejected the connections between tragedy and the ritual re-enactment of Christ's suffering ('He di'd indeed not as an actor dies') but his aesthetic sensibility was closer to Laud's than to his puritan opponents. Lamb's famous comment on the conclusion to *The Broken Heart* captures this perfectly, whilst still registering a lingering Protestant fear of the blasphemous implications:

The expression of this transcendant scene almost bears me in imagination to Calvary and the Cross: and I seem to perceive some analogy between the scenical sufferings which I am here contemplating, and the real agonies of that final completion to which I dare no more than hint a reference.[18]

7
The Broken Heart

One of the first problems to present itself in connection with *The Broken Heart* is the discrepancy between its modern critical reputation and its minimal and unsatisfactory performance history. It is common for literary critics to hail it not only as Ford's masterpiece but as one of the finest of all non-Shakespearean tragedies. Yet it was the only one of Ford's major plays not to be revived before the end of the nineteenth century, and it has still not, at the time of writing, had a satisfactory modern performance. Prior to the RSC's decision to include it in their 1994 autumn programme, the one professional revival had been directed by Laurence Olivier at Chichester in 1962, and its relative lack of success (the *Spectator* called it a 'painful evening' and *The Times* spoke of 'a slight sense of let-down . . . not from the production but from the play') seems to have discouraged further attempts to repeat the experiment.[1] Moreover, the terms in which the play is frequently praised ('in *The Broken Heart* we have the nearest English approach to the pure form of French classical tragedy') do not make it sound particularly appealing to English theatrical tastes.[2] It would be easy to conclude that here we have a simple opposition between literary and dramatic valuations, with the quality of Ford's poetry ensuring a continued critical interest in a theatrical dodo. In fact, *The Broken Heart* is probably particularly dependent for its special emotional effect on the full resources of theatre, including the use of music and ritual action, though whether it will ever get the production it deserves remains an open question.

Its title indicates that it is centrally preoccupied with tragic emotions ('The title lends no expectation here / Of apish laughter') and it is the way in which these emotions are represented, articulated or suppressed which makes Ford at times seem peculiarly 'modern' whilst, in more historical terms, illuminating some of the contradictory consequences of Senecan influence on English Renaissance drama. The model for tragedy presented to the Elizabethans by Seneca was one in which extreme passions, frequently bordering on madness, were given extensive rhetorical elaboration and amplification. The capacity of tragedies to move their audiences was a corollary of the capacity of their poetic language to express extreme psychological states. Yet alongside this highly emotive and rhetorical Senecan dramatic inheritance came a set of ethical ideals deriving more from Seneca the Stoic philosopher than Seneca the tragedian. The philosophical essays and letters argued consistently that virtue and contentment were only to be found in rational self-control and the total suppression of grief, fear and all other passions. Seneca seems to have realised that if the protagonists of his tragedies had followed his philosophical dictates, then the emotional basis of tragedy, its special claim to our attention, would have been destroyed. Hence he was content to let his tragedies function mainly as negative exempla rather than as direct vehicles of his Stoic views.

Prior to Ford, a number of English dramatists (pre-eminently Chapman and Marston) had attempted a more direct presentation of Stoic ideals within the form of tragedy. An obvious dramatic problem arises, in so far as the more completely successful characters are in achieving a calm control over their emotions, the less tragic they appear. For an audience to feel pity for characters attempting to live by Stoic ideals, it is necessary either for the carefully cultivated indifference to misfortune to crumble catastrophically under the pressure of events – Marston's 'Man will break out, despite philosophy' (*Antonio's Revenge*, IV. v. 46) is the classic expression of this – or for the dramatist to find ways of intimating the strength of the emotions which have been brought under control and the difficulty and cost of their continued suppression. Ford's play revolves round this dual Senecan inheritance of extreme tragic passions and the conscious attempt to suppress them, but he also, at times, seems to anticipate psychoanalytic insights into the processes of *unconscious* repression. Moreover, another Senecan notion developed by Ford – that there may be griefs too great for rhetorical expression – foreshadows a good deal of post-Romantic agonising over the inadequacies of verbal representation and permits a critic like Harriet Hawkins to claim that *The Broken Heart* 'has at least as many affinities with the Romantic-Symbolic-Imagistic-Impressionistic-Expressionistic-Modernist traditions of poetry and drama as it has with the works of Ford's own contemporaries and precursors'.[3]

The entire action of the play is shaped by events which took place before it opened – the annulment of Penthea's betrothal to Orgilus by her brother Ithocles and her subsequent forced marriage to the old and jealous Bassanes. This basic situation is the breeding ground for a number of feelings which are given fairly full expression. 'My griefs are violent', declares Orgilus in the first scene, and his father later rebukes him for 'the wolf of hatred snarling in your breast' (III. v. 33). The jealousy of Bassanes is also given free vent to the extent that in the first half of the play he seems more like a Jonsonian 'humour' than a dignified nobleman. Yet the setting for these burning passions is Sparta, a state which resembled Rome in the range of connotations it possessed for the Renaissance. Spartan values, like Roman ones, were military, patriotic, ascetic, virile and broadly Stoic ones. The prime virtues included devotion to duty and the capacity to endure pain. In the note accompanying his chosen extracts from *The Broken Heart*, Lamb refers to the famous and proverbial courage 'of the Spartan boy who let a beast gnaw out his bowels till he died without expressing a groan'.[4] Although Orgilus successfully enacts his revenge upon Ithocles, the characters' emotions do not swell towards an explosive and expressive violence. Rather, a Stoic control and aristocratic dignity reasserts itself and pervades the final moments of both men. Ithocles' courage, as he is murdered in the trick chair, clearly echoes that of Webster's Flamineo, similarly trapped and unable to fight back:

> Strike home! A courage
> As keen as thy revenge shall give it welcome.
> But prithee faint not; if the wound close up,
> Tent it with double force and search it deeply.
> Thou looks that I should whine and beg compassion . . .
>
> (IV. iv. 39–43)

Taken out of context the lines could easily pass for Webster's, but, for my argument, it is more important to emphasise the differences of dramatic effect. Ithocles is able to assume his stance easily and with complete success. There is an assured Spartan heroism which is impressive but hardly moving. With Flamineo, however, Webster makes us far more aware of the emotional fluctuations which accompany his bravado, of the emptiness and horror just beneath the surface, of the terrible effort of will involved. Webster's jagged, discontinuous style is more able to capture the *process* of trying to die bravely. Ford presents us instead with the picture of a successfully achieved mastery over fear.

Similarly, the protracted bleeding to death of Orgilus, for all the grisly interest the staging of such a spectacle might provoke, has a curiously detached quality about it (the scene was cut completely from William Poel's 1898 production). Orgilus is so in charge of his emotions ('look upon my steadiness') that there is no opportunity for the audience to engage theirs. The 'tragic' quality of the scene is of a largely formal and self-consciously literary kind:

> This pastime
> Appears majestical; some high-tun'd poem
> Hereafter shall deliver to posterity
> The writer's glory and his subject's triumph.
>
> (V. ii. 130–3)

For a modern audience, and probably a seventeenth-century one too, the emotional centre of *The Broken Heart* is to be found not in its heroic male characters but in Penthea and Calantha, the two women who must also try to live by Sparta's codes of honour and self-control.[5] That these codes are essentially masculine ones, and that they will therefore exact a greater, a more truly tragic price from the women who follow them, is indicated by Calantha's reference to the Spartan habit of only accepting male kings:

> A woman has enough to govern wisely
> Her own demeanours, passions, and divisions.
> A nation warlike and inur'd to practice
> Of policy and labour cannot brook
> A feminate authority.
>
> (V. iii. 8–12)

Within this Spartan world of military honour and heroic feats of endurance Ford has established his two main female characters as strongly opposed types, Penthea being the more conventionally 'feminine' personality, whilst Calantha is more assertive, regal and 'masculine'. Both, however, are capable of exerting an iron control over their emotions when necessary, though Penthea's softer nature makes the processes of mental conflict involved more intense and dramatic. Deprived of the man she loves and 'buried in a bride-bed' (a phrase as resonant as Blake's 'marriage-hearse'), she is central to the play's four most affecting scenes – her meeting and parting with Orgilus (II. iii), her 'reconciliation' with her brother Ithocles (III. iii), her pleading of her brother's cause to Calantha (III. vi) and her final madness (IV. ii). In the first three of these scenes she struggles successfully to contain her natural feelings, though their pressure is evident in details of language and action. When Orgilus reveals his identity, she clasps his hand with both of hers, kisses it and kneels before him. When he kneels too, all the intimate formality of their betrothal is touchingly re-enacted, but only as the prelude to a final separation:

> We may stand up. Have you ought else to urge
> Of new demand? As for the old, forget it;
> 'Tis buried in an everlasting silence,
> And shall be, shall be ever.
>
> (II. iii. 67–70)

The physical and emotional space she establishes between them ('Remove / Your steps some distance from me') is dramatically bridged in the mad scene when she once again seeks out his hand, clasps it in hers, kisses it and in all probability (though there is no explicit stage direction) kneels again to Orgilus (IV. ii. 110ff). The dialogue implies that he at first flinches from the contact, no doubt because he remembers her desire to be subjected to an even worse fate than her current marriage 'If of all the men alive thou shouldst but touch / My lip or hand again' (II. iii. 106–7). The collapse of her self-denying resolution into a renewed physical intimacy has the force of a broken ritual but also of a reaffirmed one.

Penthea can be seen as a deeper and fuller version of the type of lovelorn maiden common in Jacobean and Caroline drama, but she is distinguished from the norm by her corrosive self-hatred. She describes her marital relations with Bassanes as a form of adultery and sees herself as a 'faith breaker' and a 'spotted whore'. The marriage was 'A rape done on my truth' (II. iii. 79) but like many victims of rape she feels physically polluted and therefore morally tainted herself. Her decision to starve herself to death, although 'mad' in one sense, is perfectly logical in another. It satisfies her deep impulses towards self-punishment whilst carrying strong religious connotations of purification through fasting (compare the Duchess of Malfi's 'The Church enjoins fasting: / I'll starve myself to death' – IV. i. 75–6). The impression of powerfully ambivalent feelings which remain imperfectly articulated is so strong in the case of Penthea that a psychoanalytic approach begins to look more rewarding than is usually the case with Ford.

Previous links between Ford and Freud have generally been made on the misleading basis that both exemplify a scientific and amoral approach to psychological problems. One might, with more justice, argue instead that both have a highly developed tragic sense of life, that both emphasise the necessary but harsh price which any form of civilisation exacts from human beings, and that both are capable of a particularly rigorous form of compassion. There are plenty of allusions in *The Broken Heart* to 'silent griefs', 'hidden wounds' and conflicting feelings ('What can you look for. . . but language suited to a divided mind?' – I. iii. 64–7) but the encouragement these offer to psychoanalytic approaches may be rather deceptive. In general, the emotions of Ford's characters are not especially mysterious either to themselves or to the audience. One only needs to contrast the treatment of incestuous attraction in *'Tis Pity She's a Whore* with that in *The Duchess of Malfi* to see how it is Webster rather than Ford who seems to be suggesting that there may be unconscious mental processes at work. Ford is normally more concerned with desires and conflicts at a conscious level, feelings clear though deep. His language may suggest that much is submerged, but, like icebergs, the nature of what is submerged is not seriously in doubt.

Penthea, however, is more complicated than this. The self-hatred which distinguishes her from other bereaved lovers in Renaissance drama is the specific factor which Freud uses to differentiate pathological melancholia from 'normal' mourning for a lost love-object:

> The melancholic displays something else besides which is lacking in mourning – an extraordinary diminution in his self-regard, an impoverishment of his ego on a grand scale. In mourning it is the world which has become poor and empty; in melancholia it is the ego itself. The patient represents his ego to us as worthless, incapable of any achievement and morally despicable; he reproaches himself, vilifies himself and expects to be cast out and punished. . . . This picture of a delusion of (mainly moral) inferiority is completed by sleeplessness and refusal to take nourishment, and – what is psychologically very remarkable – by an overcoming of the instinct which compels every living thing to cling to life.[6]

Much of this, of course, differs little from what Ford would have found in Burton's *Anatomy of Melancholy*, but Freud goes significantly beyond Burton in arguing that the key to this clinical picture is that 'the self-reproaches are reproaches against a loved object which have been shifted away from it on to the patient's own ego'.[7] In other words, it is not simply Penthea's loss of Orgilus but her resentment against Ithocles which is responsible for her condition. Unable to direct her hatred fully at a once loved brother, it is displaced partly onto herself. According to Freud, this process is more likely to occur if the original love relationship involved a high degree of narcissistic identification, and it is not immaterial that halfway through the play it is revealed that Penthea and Ithocles were in fact twins. Even Bassanes grotesque suspicions of incest, made slightly less ridiculous by our knowledge of *'Tis Pity*, may serve to hint at the original strength of feeling between brother and sister, as well as serving the primary function of demonstrating the pathological excesses of his jealousy.

Penthea's ambivalent feelings towards Ithocles complicate her role as victim, unconsciously fuelling her self-hatred but also generating a kind of passive aggression which manifests itself in various ways. It is well known that suicide may combine a desire for self-punishment with a desire to hurt others, and the philosopher Tecnicus, speaking in another context, provides the appropriate gloss on Penthea's self-starvation when he argues that 'They care not / For harms to others who contemn their own' (I. iii. 17–18). Even when nobly pleading Ithocles love to Calantha, Penthea cannot prevent herself adding, impulsively and potentially damagingly, that 'this brother / Hath been, you know, unkind; O, most unkind!' (III. vi. 105–6). Her earlier generous *rapprochement* with Ithocles ('We are reconciled') was itself not altogether free from a suggestion of satisfaction that he was now equal with her in misery. This ambivalence reaches its climax in the mad scene in which her first line is the cryptic 'Sure, if we were all sirens we should sing pitifully' (IV. ii. 69). As well as conveying a Prufrock-like frustrated romanticism, this perhaps also hints longingly at the capacity of the sirens to draw men to their deaths. This hint is made concrete in the action which ensues when, in the middle of her pathetic ramblings, Penthea points out Ithocles: 'But that is he. . . . That's he, and still 'tis he.' It is a highly dramatic moment, comparable to Lavinia in *Titus Andronicus* scratching the names of her violators in the sand, and though Penthea still cannot directly express any hatred or desire for revenge, her gesture can have only one meaning for Orgilus ('She has tutor'd me').

The preceding analysis of Penthea does more justice to the subtlety of Ford's psychology than simply emphasising her pathos as a victim, but pathos remains the primary emotion aimed at, the pathos of a woman who combines the vulnerability of childhood and old age without ever having enjoyed a fulfilled adult existence. She says to Calantha that 'though I am much old in griefs, / In years I am a child' (III. vi. 50–1) and makes the same point even more affectingly in her mad speeches:

> But 'tis too late for me to marry now,
> I am past child-bearing; 'tis not my fault.
> (IV. ii. 93–4)

The childish "'tis not my fault' which succeeds her lament for a wasted life is a brilliant touch.

In complete contrast to this all-too-evident and 'feminine' vulnerability, Calantha maintains a Stoic and 'masculine spirit' to the very end. Unlike Penthea, she repeatedly asserts herself to make sure she succeeds in marrying the man she loves. She first meets Ithocles when she crowns him with the victor's laurel wreath, a moment whose physical intimacy gives greater plausibility to the convention of instant mutual attraction. She then proceeds to forward their relationship by a number of decisive gestures. She takes his arm at the end of III. iv, rebuffing her official suitor Nearchus with 'Nay, good / My lord, keep on your way; I am provided' (75–6). She subsequently denies her ring to Nearchus, throwing it with apparent casualness to Ithocles, and then directly asks her father for Ithocles to be placed in her service. Even when apparently robbed of her husband by Orgilus' revenge, her indomitable will insists on performing the marriage ceremony and she places her ring on the dead man's finger:

> Thus I new marry him whose wife I am;
> Death shall not separate us.
> (V. iii. 66–7)

The same strength of will manifests itself in the regal and Stoic calm with which she responds to the news of 'death, and death, and death', refusing to interrupt the preordained sequence of the dance. The conscious control of emotion here comes close to seeming inhuman and the sparse evidence from actual performances suggests that the scene is difficult to bring off. The Revels edition of the play records one spectator of a 1904 production as being 'distinctly unimpressed by the tragedy – *especially* by the much-praised penultimate scene, which went very flat'.[8] It is apt

to seem strange to the audience as well as the onstage characters
that 'these tragedies should never touch on / Her female pity'
(V. ii. 93–4) and the consequence can easily be that 'the ritual
keeps us at a distance, admiring but uninvolved'.[9] For the dance
scene to work properly, we have to be fully aware of the emotions which have been successfully mastered, and Ford has
perhaps not done enough to intimate these in Calantha's previous scenes (which are mainly public ones), though much
would depend on the capabilities of the actress playing the role.
A crucial moment occurs in her interview with Penthea when
she responds to the latter's evident misery with, 'Now beshrew
thy sadness; / Thou turnst me too much woman' (III. vi. 42–3)
and begins to weep ('Her fair eyes / Melt into passion'). This
moment must not be hurried over in performance, since we need
to remember it vividly in order to feel the full tension of the
dance scene.

This tension breaks in the play's final scene to considerable
dramatic effect when we learn that Calantha's apparent calm
was not the product of Stoic reason but a courageous effort of the
will which cannot finally prevail against natural feelings:

> O, my lords,
> I but deceived your eyes with antic gesture,
> When one news straight came huddling on another
> Of death, and death, and death. Still I danc'd forward,
> But it struck home, and here, and in an instant. . .
> They are the silent griefs which cut the heartstrings;
> Let me die smiling.
>
> (V. iii. 67–76)

Ford undoubtedly intended these final moments to be highly
emotional. The hard-won self-control of Bassanes ('Mark me,
nobles, / I do not shed a tear, not for Penthea') breaks down
again in a way which is meant to represent the inevitable audience response: 'I must weep to see / Her smile in death' (V. iii.
97–8). A modern reader who, unlike Lamb, finds Ford's language
insufficiently expressive to achieve the desired aim should
ponder the aesthetic implications of the Senecan phrase which
lies behind Calantha's 'They are the silent griefs which cut the

heartstrings.' Despite his taste for rhetorical excess, Seneca included in the *Phaedra* a counter-proposition which was to fascinate English dramatists: '*Curae leves loquuntur, ingentes stupent*' ('Light sorrows speak out, great ones render us dumb'). Isabella's line in *The White Devil*, '*Those are the killing griefs which dare not speak*' (II. i. 277), is only one of many such rephrasings of the basic concept. Despite being opposed character types, both Penthea and Calantha appear to possess feelings too full for verbal expression. The odd phrase Orgilus uses of Penthea, that she 'is left a prey to words' (IV. ii. 44), seems to hint, if it is not simply a misprint, at this radical disjunction of language and feeling. If one asks how a verbal medium is able to represent emotions which are 'beyond words', then the obvious answer is that theatre is much more than a verbal medium. In addition to the expressive gestures and vocal tones of his actors, Ford was able to make considerable use of music to suggest thoughts and feelings which lie too deep for language.

The stage directions refer explicitly to four songs and two pieces of instrumental music but one should not forget the preliminary and inter-act music which was a normal part of indoor theatre performances. The degree to which this was used to create specific moods relating to the emotional fluctuations of particular plays is uncertain but it is an expressive possibility which is left undeveloped in most modern productions of what were originally 'private' theatre plays. It is of some significance that all the music directly mentioned in the text occurs in the second half of the play. As the emotional pressure rises, Ford seems to be trying to push beyond the limitations of the imitative arts. The first words of the first song are '*Can you paint a thought?*' (III. ii. 1) which echoes Hieronymo's 'mad' question about art and anguish in one of the 1602 additions to *The Spanish Tragedy* ('Canst paint a doleful cry?'). In his introduction to the nineteenth-century Mermaid selection of Ford's plays, Havelock Ellis spoke of how Ford 'strained the limits of his art to the utmost; he forboded new ways of expression'.[10] Writing on Ford in the twentieth century, Clifford Leech also spoke of how 'in art there is continually a reaching towards that mode of perception which the chosen art-form does not easily allow', but he developed this into an argument that Ford's distinctiveness lay in trying to turn the temporal art of drama into something static and pictorial:

'Defying the natural limitations of drama, Ford aims at a form of spatial perception. When we first read his plays, what remains most persistently in our minds is a series of static groupings.'[11]

No one would wish to dispute that *The Broken Heart* has many scenes in which the characters are carefully grouped emblematically rather than moving and interacting freely, but the art-form which the play is straining towards, the art-form best capable of intimating hidden griefs, seems to me to be music rather than painting. Ford seemed 'modern' to Havelock Ellis not just because of his psychological acuteness but because he exemplified the post-Romantic view that 'All art constantly aspires towards the condition of music'.[12] The most pertinent version of this idea occurs in Nietzsche's *The Birth of Tragedy*, where a Platonic distrust of 'appearance' and 'imitation' is developed into a celebration of music rather than rational discourse as the best means of access to the world as it really is:

The world-symbolism of music cannot be exhaustively interpreted through language, because it symbolically refers to the primal contradiction and the primal suffering within the primal Oneness, and thus symbolizes a sphere beyond and prior to all phenomena. In comparison with this, all phenomena are mere symbols: hence *language*, as the organ and symbol of phenomena, can never uncover the innermost core of music.[13]

Although tragedy was born from the spirit of music, 'music is the actual idea of the world, drama a mere reflection of that idea, an isolated silhouette of it'.[14] As an imitative art concerned with appearances, drama cannot, in Nietzsche's terms, express 'primal contradiction' and 'primal suffering' so well as music. In *The Broken Heart*, the songs, the instrumental music and the cadences of Ford's verse all seem to be straining beyond the limits of verbal representation to express the killing griefs which dare not, or *cannot*, speak. In this respect his art is 'melodramatic' in the original and precise sense of the word rather than in its later and more pejorative usage.

Seeing Ford's play in terms of Nietzsche's theories of music and tragedy is illuminating up to a point, but it risks being seriously misleading if pushed too far. Nietzsche spoke of 'primal contradiction' and 'primal suffering' and 'the radical "pity of

things"' but he combined this with exuberant claims for music
and tragedy as assertions of the eternal life of the will: "'We believe in eternal life" is tragedy's cry; while music is the
immediate idea of that life.'[15] By contrast, Ford's music, poetry,
and action seem to be geared to express a more passive and melancholy sense of death as the inevitable, and even desired, goal
of existence. This note had been sounded frequently in Ford's
earlier works:

> He that remembers that he lives a life, cannot but fore-thinke
> that he must die a death: If hee looke into what life it selfe is,
> hee shall finde (by experience of the past, and the proofe of
> the present age) that it is none other but a journey to death. If
> a man examine the scope of his owne desires, they will fall out
> to be a desiring to hasten to his grave.[16]

Penthea is the chief vehicle for such sentiments in *The Broken
Heart* but she is only articulating a mood which gradually pervades the whole play:

> In vain we labour in this course of life
> To piece our journey out at length, or crave
> Respite of breath; our home is in the grave.
> (II. iii. 145–7)

From such a perspective, human attempts to defy the passage of
time and the coming of death take on an air of ironic futility. The
play begins with the aged Spartan king making just such an
attempt:

> See, lords, Amyclas your old king is ent'ring
> Into his youth again. I shall shake off
> This silver badge of age, and change this snow
> For hairs as gay as are Apollo's locks.
> Our heart leaps in new vigour.
> (I. ii. 4–8)

The degree of dramatic irony involved here depends on how obviously decrepit the actor is made to look, but, by Act IV,
Amyclas has been overcome by sickness and has to be supported

by his courtiers and placed in a chair (chairs are important prop-
erties in *The Broken Heart* and we will shortly see both Penthea
and Ithocles sitting dead in their chairs). He still appears to have
hopes of cheating death:

> There is no physic
> So currently restorative to cherish
> The fall of age, or call back youth and vigour,
> As your consents in duty. I will shake off
> This languishing disease of time. . .
>
> (IV. iii. 51–5)

However, the grammar of the first sentence is such that, before
it completes itself, the absolute impossibility of these hopes has
been grimly articulated.

The manner in which Orgilus is bled to death, standing rather
than sitting, is probably meant to recall Chapman's Bussy D'Ambois who also died standing, propped on his sword in a pose of
heroic constancy ('I am up / Here like a Roman statue; I will
stand / Till death hath made me marble' – V. iii. 143–5). However, the fact that Orgilus is supported by two staves makes him
emblematic of old age and frailty as well as Stoic heroism. When
his veins are empty, he totters feebly, before, in all probability,
collapsing to the ground with a spectacular crash:

> When feeble man is bending to his mother,
> The dust 'a was first fram'd on, thus he totters.
>
> (V. ii. 147–8)

As well as signifying the inevitable defeat of the will, the action
also carries suggestions of a desired return to the bosom of
mother earth, to the peace of oblivion. Stoic philosophy could be
seen as ambiguously celebrating both the assertion of the individual's will and a sacrifice of that will to cosmic 'necessity',
resulting in something resembling the death drive speculated
about by Freud in *Beyond the Pleasure Principle*, the drive to return
to an earlier, inorganic state of being.[17] Both implications are
probably present in the death of Orgilus and are also to be found
in other aspects of the play. The fidelity to their vows of both
Penthea and Calantha, and the attempts of all the characters to

maintain self-control, help to give them their sense of personal identity, help to define them against the flow of time and the nullity of death. There is little doubt that Ford was highly sympathetic to these ideals of constancy. *The Broken Heart* was the first of four plays to carry the anagram which he devised from his own name, 'Fide Honor' (Honour through Fidelity). Yet *The Broken Heart* also strongly suggests that the Stoic values of constancy and self-control can be seen as a commitment to death as much as a triumph over it. Penthea's vows confer identity upon her but destroy her. Calantha is literally, and with great ceremony, married to death at the end of the play. The Stoic control of emotion comes to seem little different from death itself:

> Welcome, thou ice that sitt'st about my heart;
> No heat can ever thaw thee.
>
> (V. ii. 153–4)

The total emotional effect of the play, realisable only through the full resources of theatre, results in something much more complex than the endorsement of a particular ethical position. Ford's 'still sad music' expresses a desire for oblivion as much as the 'eternal life of the will' or, more precisely, suggests that the two amount to the same thing.

8

'Tis Pity She's a Whore

In comparison with *The Broken Heart*, *'Tis Pity She's a Whore* has been less consistently praised by literary critics but has a much stronger stage history. A note at the end of the 1633 Quarto speaks of 'the general commendation deserved by the actors in their presentment of this tragedy' and in 1639 it was included in a list of plays belonging to the Cockpit theatre which its new manager William Beeston, son of Christopher, wished to protect from other acting companies. This was presumably a mark of its continued commercial viability and its reputation was enough to ensure it at least two revivals soon after the Restoration. The absence of any further productions until the twentieth century is attributable more to moral objections to its subject matter than to doubts about its theatrical effectiveness. The liberalisation of moral attitudes in the 1960s has resulted in a steady stream of both amateur and professional productions since 1968, including heavily adapted versions for film and television. Writing before he had the benefit of seeing many of these, the editor of the Revels edition was nevertheless confident that 'few Jacobean tragedies outside Shakespeare stand up so well to revival'.[1] The opportunity to see and compare a number of subsequent performances has helped to confirm the play's theatrical power, which now seems beyond dispute, and to clarify some unex-

pected strengths, such as the effectiveness of the scenes involving Bergetto and the importance of other 'minor' characters like
Vasques. Not all recent productions have been equally successful, but when fine actors have been well directed, as in David
Leveaux's production for the RSC at the Swan in 1991, the result
has been shattering.

Ranking *'Tis Pity* below both *The Broken Heart* and *Perkin
Warbeck*, T. S. Eliot argued that the play lacked 'general significance and emotional depth' and that 'this defect separates it
completely from the best plays of Webster, Middleton and
Tourneur'.[2] It is easy to suspect that there is a concealed moral
point being made here and that Eliot's lack of 'general significance' is simply a diluted version of earlier and more direct
objections to the topic of brother–sister incest, such as that of
Charles Dibdin, writing at the end of the eighteenth century: 'It
is not the province of a dramatic writer to seek for monsters, and
to record prodigies; it is his duty to reprehend such vices as
are commonly known, and often practised.'[3] Such a critical position would rule out a large proportion of the world's most
admired tragedies, beginning with *Oedipus Rex*, but in any case
the charge that *'Tis Pity* lacks general significance seems particularly ill-founded. Many plays dramatise a conflict between the
individual's desires and society's moral code, but often in ways
that are culturally very specific. Sophocles' *Antigone* turns on the
heroine's defiance of the king her father's refusal to allow her
brother 'proper' burial. Since we also prefer our relatives to
be buried or cremated, we have little difficulty in empathising
with her position, but it would have seemed strange to Sophocles' Persian contemporaries whose Zoroastrian religion forbade
corpses to be buried or burned. Sophocles was able to transform
culturally specific forms of behaviour into an enduring myth of
the individual's conflict with the state, capable of being invoked
and reworked in many different contexts. The nature of the taboo
which Giovanni and Annabella violate makes it even easier for
Ford to achieve this 'general significance'.

Although we have probably lost a sense of the special social
importance which brother–sister relationships possessed in earlier, more patriarchal societies (both Webster and Ford seem
fascinated by this particular relationship and its possibilities for
abuse), we have not lost the deeply ingrained revulsion from in-

cest which Ford would have assumed in his audience. For the structuralist anthropologist Claude Lévi-Strauss, the incest taboo was a rare example of a genuine cultural universal. The structures of different kinship systems, the different 'languages' of social relations, could be understood only in relation to this universal prohibition.[4] Lévi-Strauss exaggerated the degree of universality involved but, nevertheless, the widespread and deeply felt horror aroused by incest means that the breaking of this taboo is particularly suited to represent *all* fundamental challenges to religious, moral and social authority. A modern audience feels the force of Giovanni's challenge to society more directly and viscerally in the achieved incestuous relationship than in the gestures towards atheism which accompany it.

The principle representative of moral orthodoxy in the play is the Friar and it is important to try and decide what kind of authority Ford intends him to have. For an English Protestant audience such figures must have always been potentially ambiguous, capable of signifying corrupt Catholicism as well as conventional moral wisdom. Shakespeare's Friar in *Romeo and Juliet* is presented in straightforwardly positive terms, but his equivalent in Chapman's *Bussy D'Ambois* is a much more dubious figure, who facilitates an adulterous relationship and raises spirits from the underworld, whilst still being used by Chapman from time to time in a choric role. Some critics have found Ford's Friar harsh and unsympathetic, especially in his attempt to terrify Annabella into repentance (III. vi), but there is genuine warmth in his relations with the lovers ('The more I hear, I pity thee the more') and an anguished concern for their spiritual welfare ('This grieves me most, / Things being thus, a pair of souls are lost' – II. v. 68–9). The knowledge that some of the details of his hellfire speech to Annabella come from Ford's own religious poem *Christes Bloodie Sweat* merely helps to confirm that the Friar's views, articulating the full weight of traditional religious opposition to incest, whether Catholic or Protestant, are meant to be taken seriously.

It is true that at two points he compromises his moral authority, first by recommending promiscuous fornication to Giovanni as the lesser of two evils ('Leave her, and take thy choice; 'tis much less sin' – I. i. 62), and secondly by telling Annabella, for her 'honour's safety', to marry Soranzo, whose adulterous affair with Hippolita appears to have been well known in Parma. In each case he shows the kind of pragmatism necessary for social existence, a pragmatism which must inevitably appear hypocritical to a romantic absolutist like Giovanni but which, in its concern to make the best of a terrible situation, cannot be dismissed as merely cynical. In Griffi's 1973 film version, the Friar is given much less to say (there is no repentance scene with Annabella) and appears at first to lack the authority he has in the play (in one of the opening shots he appears to be at Giovanni's feet rather than in the dominant relation of teacher to pupil). However, he does not make any moral compromises. The advice to marry Soranzo comes from an ecclesiastical superior and, disgusted by it, he leaves the monastery to which he was attached in order to live away from society, poor but honest. However well intentioned Ford's Friar may be, he lacks this kind of absolute spiritual integrity to set against the absolute romantic values of Giovanni. He remains part of society, part of the same church as the Cardinal, who protects the murderer Grimaldi, orders the blinded Putana to be burnt, and seizes all the Florio household's gold and jewels into the possession of the Pope. He might also be criticised for his abdication of responsibility at the end of the play ('back to Bononia I / With speed will haste and shun this coming blow') but the main point of this departure is to symbolise that Giovanni is now beyond hope ('I leave thee to despair') and to create a sense of inevitable doom similar to that evoked when the Good Angel leaves Doctor Faustus.

The many verbal and situational echoes of Marlowe's play, some of which were first pointed out by Cyrus Hoy, are very important to Ford in helping to give his story some of the universal resonance of the Faust myth, some of the 'general significance' which Eliot found lacking in *'Tis Pity*.[5] Like Faustus, Giovanni is a brilliant scholar at a famous European university. His 'wit' and 'art' bring him up against the limits of traditional thinking and his cleverness means that he is never short of arguments with which to rationalise his desires. Again, like Faustus, this cleverness masks fundamental confusions and inconsistencies. Faustus is able to deny the reality of hell in the manner of a sophisticated freethinker ('Come, I think hell's a fable') whilst in the process of seeking power from the devil. Giovanni likewise denies hell when it suits him:

> Now I can tell you
> The hell you oft have prompted, is nought else
> But slavish and fond, superstitious fear;
> And I could prove it too –
>
> (V. iii. 18–21)

However, he seems pathetically anxious to believe Annabella's assurances of an afterlife and, when he kills her, seems to imagine that he is sending her to paradise:

> Go thou white in thy soul to fill a throne
> Of innocence and sanctity in Heaven.
>
> (V. v. 64–5)

Giovanni and Faustus both have a tendency to violent mood swings, but whereas Faustus begins in a state of arrogant over-confidence before ending in despair, Giovanni proceeds from abject hopelessness (the 1991 RSC production began with him sprawled tearfully on the floor) to an exultant hubris which places him beyond reach of any human being, even Annabella. More positively, both men also have an intense responsiveness to beauty and a capacity to express more than merely material aspirations. This 'spiritual' side to their natures coexists rather oddly with the gestures towards a materialist and 'naturalist' philosophy of the kind more consistently expressed by figures like D'Amville, the protagonist of Tourneur's *The Atheist's Tragedy* (c.1611), or Edmund in Shakespeare's *King Lear*.

Rather than making the orthodox Renaissance identification of 'natural' law with moral and religious teaching, D'Amville and Edmund argue for an essentially amoral conception of Nature in which it is only 'natural' for men to try to satisfy their urges, whatever these may be. D'Amville explicitly characterises the incest prohibition as 'against Nature':

> Incest, tush!
> These distances affinity observes
> Are articles of bondage cast upon

> Our freedoms by our own subjections.
> Nature allows a gen'ral liberty
> Of generation to all creatures else.
> Shall man, to whose command and use all creatures
> Were made subject, be less free than they?
>   (IV. iii. 123–30)

In *'Tis Pity* this view is given its crudest form of expression by
Putana, Annabella's 'tut'ress': 'What though he be your brother?
Your brother's a man I hope, and I say still, if a young wench
feel the fit upon her, let her take anybody, father or brother, all is
one' (II. i. 43–6). Delivered correctly, the lines are capable of getting a laugh in the theatre, but if Ford had allowed his lovers to
speak in these terms they would have forfeited most of their
claims to our sympathy. Giovanni does indeed invoke Nature in
his defence, but does so in more refined language as part of an
impassioned claim to spiritual and intellectual as well as physical affinity:

> Are we not therefore each to other bound
> So much the more by nature, by the links
> Of blood, of reason – nay, if you will have't,
> Even of religion – to be ever one,
> One soul, one flesh, one love, one heart, one all?
>   (I. i. 30–4)

It is impossible to ignore the emotional appeal of this romantic
rhetoric, and by provocatively raising the whole question of 'the
nature of Nature', the question which is at the heart of *King Lear*,
'Tis Pity aspires to some of the 'general significance' of Shakespeare's play.

We continue to pose modern versions of the same question
but the form in which it appears in Ford, that of a potential
schism between Nature and God, is very typical of the intellectual upheavals of the seventeenth century. The sense of a deep
and developing split between different kinds of knowledge, different kinds of truth, was a major characteristic of the period and
this is exemplified most powerfully by some lines in which it is
the Friar rather than Giovanni who appears to concede that incest
might conceivably be justified as natural and reasonable. He re-

sponds to Giovanni's Neoplatonic arguments with this highly significant outburst:

> O ignorance in knowledge! Long ago,
> How often have I warn'd thee this before?
> Indeed, if we were sure there were no Deity,
> Nor Heaven nor Hell, then to be led alone
> By Nature's light – as were philosophers
> Of elder times – might instance some defence.
> But 'tis not so. Then, madman, thou wilt find
> That Nature is in Heaven's positions blind.
>   (II. v. 27–34)[6]

Previously in English Renaissance drama, only an atheist libertine like D'Amville would have attempted to argue that incest was 'natural'. In *Hamlet* and *The Revenger's Tragedy* the notion of incest is used to intensify a more general sexual disgust by evoking the horror of the unnatural. In *The Duchess of Malfi* the hints of incestuous attraction are part of a consistent characterisation of Ferdinand as sinister and perverse. However, the beginnings of a scientific approach to the natural world and the revival of interest in sceptical philosophy had shaken the Christian humanist belief in the harmony of faith and reason and problematised the relations between nature, reason and God. In *Biathanatos*, probably written in 1608 though not published till 1647, John Donne attacked many of the traditional objections to suicide and argued that although the act might usually be sinful, it was not necessarily a violation of either 'the law of reason' or 'the law of nature': 'we may safely infer that nothing which we call sin is so against nature, but that it may be sometimes agreeable to nature'.[7] Similarly, the Dutch writer Hugo Grotius argued in 1625 that a number of things forbidden by God, such as fornication, incest and usury, were not necessarily contrary to natural law.[8] Donne, Grotius and Ford's Friar do not take libertine positions but they collectively exemplify a crisis in the relations between reason and faith, Nature and God. Rather than encoding and helping to demonstrate divine law, 'Nature is in Heaven's positions blind'. Giovanni, like Webster's Flamineo, seems to be faced with different and incompatible forms of knowledge which reduce him to a state of tragic confusion:

> *While we look up to heaven we confound*
> *Knowledge with knowledge.* O I am in a mist.
>   (*The White Devil*, V. vi. 257–8)

'Confusion' is a key word in Ford's play and, though capable of bearing its modern meanings of disorder or perplexity, more usually signifies death and destruction. Condemned to moral and intellectual confusion, Giovanni is also condemned to confusion in its more absolute sense.

Yet though Ford raises the possibility of a split between natural law and religious teaching, he seems also at times to imply a coincidence of the two. As in *Doctor Faustus*, there are a number of small details which suggest that the protagonist is attempting vainly to defy the natural order of the universe as much as the laws of God or society. In the scene where Soranzo courts Annabella (III. iii), Giovanni watches from above, claiming arrogantly, like a Marlovian overreacher, to be 'regent' of the fates. His power over the situation, which rests on her resolution not to marry, collapses dramatically in the face of the 'natural' sickness of early pregnancy which causes her to swoon. At that moment, Giovanni descends from his dominant position in the gallery, exclaiming significantly 'Heaven forbid!' (66). Time is one of the basic constituents of natural order and the twenty-four years during which Faustus is permitted to exercise his powers are obviously intended to symbolise the twenty-four hours of the day, which set a natural limit to human endeavours. In *'Tis Pity* this natural limit is represented by the nine months of pregnancy which mark the maximum possible duration of the incestuous relationship:

> For nine months' space in secret I enjoy'd
> Sweet Annabella's sheets; nine months I liv'd
> A happy monarch of her heart and her.
>   (V. vi. 45–7)

As his last hour began, Faustus tried in vain to stop time, to frustrate the workings of the cosmos:

Stand still, you ever-moving spheres of heaven,
That time may cease, and midnight never come.
(xiii. 62–3)

But he is forced to acknowledge his subjection to a natural order
which circumscribes his aspirations: 'The stars move still, time
runs, the clock will strike' (xiii. 69). Giovanni claims to be the
master of time and fate ('Why, I hold fate / Clasp'd in my fist,
and could command the course / Of time's eternal motion . . .' –
V. v. 11–13) but can do nothing to extend the natural limit of nine
months placed upon him and Annabella. His final murder of her
is not simply a form of romantic love-death, though it can be
staged to signify this, but an atrocity which provokes from her
the cry of 'Brother, unkind, unkind', meaning unnatural as well
as cruel. The full life-denying horror of his act becomes apparent
only when it is remembered that he is not just killing his sister
but also the unborn child inside her, and doing so in a savagely
direct manner: 'this dagger's point plough'd up / Her fruitful
womb' (V. vi. 33–4). His deed 'Darken'd the midday sun, made
noon as night' but the shocking inversion of nature which it represents would only be fully apparent in the theatre if Annabella
were visibly pregnant when she is stabbed, which is rarely the
case in modern productions.

Ford's symbolism suggests throughout that there is a natural
order more consonant with divine law than is indicated by the
Friar's 'Nature is in Heaven's positions blind'. However, there
are also other contexts and frames of reference which are important. The proliferating sub-plots help to situate Giovanni and
Annabella within a larger pattern of social relations and serve to
modify any judgement on them. It is obvious that the defects
of Annabella's three suitors – the cowardly soldier Grimaldi,
the cynical adulterer Soranzo and the idiot Bergetto – throw
Giovanni's many merits into sharp relief. Moreover, whilst the
sub-plots do not provide the kind of neat parallels with the main
plot which are regularly and rather mechanically detected and
celebrated by academic critics of Renaissance drama, they do
generate a set of variations on the themes of loyalty, betrayal,
trust, duty and service which the lovers' dangerous personal
commitment to each other forces us to reflect upon. Particularly

important are the master–servant relationships of Soranzo and Vasques, Bergetto and Poggio.

Vasques has a calm, unillusioned and sinister strength of purpose which resembles Middleton's De Flores. He is critical of his master's breach of faith to Hippolita ('You do not well, this was not your promise') but has no scruples about betraying her himself in order to protect Soranzo. He breaks his word to Putana ('my life between you and danger') in an even crueller manner, by ordering her to be blinded once he has tricked her secret out of her. Yet all this is not routine Machiavellian villainy. He tells the Cardinal bluntly at the end that 'What I have done is duty' (V. vi. 123–4), and reveals that he was a loyal servant of Soranzo's father and has continued to serve the son as faithfully as he can. He has honoured a personal commitment to the exclusion of all other moral and social obligations. He has done in his own way what Giovanni has done and there is a special irony in the way the Cardinal exempts him from serious punishment. For the RSC in 1991 Jonathan Hyde captured the character's understated menace and steely resolve perfectly.

It is possible to guess from the printed page that Vasques would turn out to be a strong acting part but less easy to see this in the case of Bergetto and his man Poggio. It is a cliché of both nineteenth- and twentieth-century criticism that Ford has no capacity for comedy and that his comic scenes are an embarrassment. Yet the reviews of most major modern productions have consistently picked out the scenes involving Bergetto for special praise. Roland Joffé's 1972 National Theatre touring production was commended for its 'genuinely funny comic scenes',[9] as was Ron Daniels's 1977 RSC production at the Other Place: 'One of the most potent factors in this utterly convincing performance is the inspired clowning of that loony ninny Bergetto.'[10] Similarly, Richard Bonneville was both funny and touching as Bergetto in the 1991 Stratford production. Bergetto has sometimes been compared to the foolish Ward in Middleton's *Women Beware Women* but he seems more closely modelled on the amiably childish Bartholomew Cokes in Jonson's *Bartholomew Fair*. A character in *The Lover's Melancholy* denies that he is 'a kind of cokes, which is, as the learned term, an ass, a puppy, a widgeon, a dolt, a noddy' (IV. ii. 181–2), all of which terms seem to fit Bergetto pretty well. His naïve enthusiasm for fairground attractions like puppet-plays and the 'strange horse . . . whose head . . . stands just behind where his tail is' (I. iii. 38–40) increases the resemblance to Jonson's great overgrown boy who loses both his purses at the fair, not to mention his hat, his coat and his sword, but is still capable of being entranced by the spectacle of the puppets. Much of the humour involving Bergetto seems simple enough, such as his inability to read his own handwriting when he wishes to declaim the contents of his love letter, but it gives a lot of scope to a good comic actor, and the implied contrast with Giovanni is not so completely favourable to the latter as one might think. Although Bergetto's manner of courtship is oafish, clumsy and utterly unromantic, he comes across as entirely inoffensive even when he is being rude. His direct, honest and unmalicious foolishness makes him what Ford's contemporaries would call 'a natural'. The word points up some of the significance of his difference from Giovanni's perverse, tortured, intensity. The social backdrop to Giovanni and Annabella's relationship includes not only the Cardinal's corruption and Soranzo's adultery but a kind of amiable, natural, ordinariness which they understandably strive to transcend but which is not wholly unattractive.

Poggio responds to his master with a mixture of dry wit, exasperation and genuine affection. The dramatic importance of the relationship came across strongly in both the RSC productions. Much of the pathos of Bergetto's death derives from the deep grief shown by his loyal servant. At the Swan in 1991, after the body had been removed, Poggio returned to retrieve Bergetto's hat left lying on the ground, and was clutching it pathetically when he exclaimed, 'O my master, my master, my master!' (III. vii. 40). At the Other Place in 1977, the final image before the interval was of Poggio alone on stage, rattling the gates of the Cardinal's house in an agony of grief and frustration. This powerful example of personal loyalty needs to be placed for comparison and contrast alongside the play's other examples of bonds and vows sustained or broken but, as Alan Dessen has said when writing of the 1977 production, 'where among the critics will the scholar find a discussion of Poggio?'[11] Modern productions of 'Tis Pity have provided repeated and irrefutable evidence of the theatrical effectiveness of these 'minor' characters and one may legitimately wonder if the uniform critical dismissal of the comic characters and scenes in Ford's other plays would would also be invalidated by the experience of actual performance.

Eliot had been prepared to concede that the death of Bergetto was 'almost pathetic' and I want to continue by challenging his claim that the play as a whole lacks 'emotional depth' as well as 'general significance'. The fact that Ford never concedes the legitimacy of the incestuous relationship precludes the kind of emotional identification with the secret lovers that Webster achieved in *The Duchess of Malfi*, but it does not preclude individual moments of great sympathy and nor is it incompatible with a sustained psychological intensity and complexity. The play's extraordinary 'balance' means that different styles of acting and direction can easily tilt our entire response one way or the other. In Philip Prowse's 1988 production for the Glasgow Citizens' Theatre, the lovers were played as 'charmless and cool',[12] whereas at the Swan in 1991, they projected a tearful emotionalism which made empathy much easier. This more emotionally open style was better able to capture and register the full range of feelings which Ford has written into the parts.[13] Giovanni is, by turns, downcast, impassioned, reverential, playful, defiant, cynical, regretful and savagely exultant; Annabella tender, warm, solemn, light-hearted, tearfully repentant, contemptuously courageous, generous and fearful. In *Hero and Leander* Marlowe wrote that 'Love is not full of pity (as men say) / But deaf and cruel where he means to prey.'[14] Ford, however, in a series of key scenes, gives us love's gentleness as well as love's cruelty, its mutual tenderness as well as its capacity for sadistic egotism.

In I. ii the pressure of unspoken feelings builds up as brother and sister circle one another uncertainly before exploding in the violent gesture with which Giovanni invites Annabella to rip open his breast and search the secrets of his heart. Less theatrical, but equally dramatic because less expected, is her revelation that the incestuous feelings are mutual ('For every sigh that thou hast spent for me, / I have sigh'd ten; for every tear, shed twenty' – I. ii. 260–1). It is not often remarked that it is *she* who initiates the unofficial betrothal ceremony which follows. As they kneel, hold hands and repeat their vows to each other, they give a touching dignity to their illicit relationship, appropriating rather than parodying the spiritual seriousness of a public ritual of commit-

ment. By contrast, Annabella's later betrothal to Soranzo is a relatively rushed affair, with briefer vows and no stage direction for
the couple to kneel. It may be more legal but the staging suggests
that it is less 'valid'. It was probably during the earlier ceremony
that Annabella gave away her mother's ring, whose absence
Florio comments on in II. vi.

A couple of other significant details require comment. The
words with which Annabella solemnly commits herself to
Giovanni are as follows:

> On my knees,
> *She kneels.*
> Brother, even by our mother's dust, I charge you,
> Do not betray me to your mirth or hate;
> Love me or kill me, brother.
>   (I. ii. 265–8)

When he repeats her words, he changes 'our mother's' to 'my
mothers'. Either Ford is quietly hinting at the more egotistical
nature of Giovanni's feelings or he is dramatising his capacity to
avoid acknowledging anything which might hinder his desires
(in this case the basic fact that they share the same mother). A
second important point is that the symbolism of the betrothal
will vary somewhat according to what happens to the dagger
which Giovanni has drawn. In Griffi's film, the lovers grasp it
mutually before letting it fall to the ground but in some stage
productions, including one directed by Jerry Turner for the
Oregon Shakespeare Festival in 1981, Giovanni continues to hold
it erect between them as they kneel, suggesting a more violent
form of eroticism and anticipating the eventual murder.

The intensity and solemnity of their betrothal changes to teas-
ing playfulness in a brief post-coital scene ('*Enter* GIOVANNI *and*
ANNABELLA, *as from their chamber*') before the relationship is left
in abeyance for some time while Ford concentrates on the sub-
plots. Isolated from each other by Ford's method of presentation,
the lovers start to follow divergent courses, Giovanni becoming
more arrogant and hubristic, whilst Annabella kneels in humility
to the Friar. Prior to the play's last two scenes, the most powerful
single episode is the post-nuptial quarrel between Soranzo and

Annabella (IV. iii). The emotional violence of this scene is as
shocking in its own way as the physical horrors of Act V.
The opening stage direction is 'Enter SORANZO *unbraced, and*
ANNABELLA *dragged in'*, and it is usual to have both characters in
some form of *déshabillé*, as if discovered in the intimacy of their
bedroom. At the Swan in 1991, Annabella was in her night-dress,
her hair flowing loose, whilst modern costuming allowed
Soranzo to be literally 'unbraced', one of his braces hanging
down off his shoulder to signify his distraught state. Annabella's
provocative defiance of her furious husband may seem surprising, given her previous penitence before the Friar, but her
growing sense of sin never shakes her love for Giovanni, or her
sense (which we partly share) of his immeasurable superiority to
a man like Soranzo. The latter's 'righteous' anger at finding her
already pregnant by another man is swelled to apoplectic fury by
her unrepentant insults:

> You! Why, you are not worthy once to name
> His name without true worship, or, indeed,
> Unless you kneel'd, to hear another name him.
>   (IV. iii. 40–3)

The emotional storm reaches its climax when she laughs and
sings in his face while he drags her round the stage by her hair.
Despite the disturbing viciousness of Soranzo's behaviour, there
is undeniably something peculiarly thrilling in seeing the hitherto gentle Annabella's surge of defiant courage. This sudden
revelation of unexpected qualities in a character is more typical
of Webster than Ford and the impression of very real and human
inconsistency is increased by her softer emotional response when
Soranzo's rage appears to subside into tearful protestations of his
love for her. She exclaims, 'O my lord! / These words wound
deeper than your sword could do' (IV. iii. 131–2) and tries to
kneel to him. The emotional 'balance' of the scene depends a
good deal on how Soranzo is played, which can vary consider-
ably in different productions. He can be a brutal hypocrite,
whose gentler words are merely Machiavellian temporising, or
(as in the case of Tim McInnerny at the Swan in 1991) he can appear genuinely bewildered and weepy, 'a shy, slightly gauche
man-about-town' who 'is left no option but to become embroiled

in the general butchery – the victim of a society which, despite its formal relationship with the church, has no absolute values'.[15] Although this latter reading seems to go against the text at a number of points, it proved a surprisingly convincing way of playing this key scene.

Annabella's emotional fluctuations contrast with Giovanni's increasingly psychotic fixity of purpose. She generously wishes that all the punishment for their sin might fall on her alone and strives to save his life, despite knowing there is no escape for herself. He, meanwhile, perversely dismisses the warning letter written in her blood as forged, though he had, moments earlier, acknowledged it as being in her hand. Their last scene together is highly charged and much depends on the precise manner in which it is staged. It opens with them lying on a bed and the dialogue makes it clear that Annabella, for the first time since her marriage, has refused to make love with Giovanni. After an outburst of jealous cynicism, in which he accuses her of finding more sophisticated sexual pleasures with Soranzo than he was capable of providing, he accuses her of breaking her vows to him: 'Thou art a faithless sister' (V. v. 9). If one were to argue that such vows are more honoured in the breach than in the observance, one would be embarrassingly echoing Soranzo's cynical words to his discarded mistress Hippolita:

> The vows I made – if you remember well –
> Were wicked and unlawful; 'twere more sin
> To keep them than to break them; as for me,
> I cannot mask my penitence.
> (II. ii. 87–90)

Giovanni, in his apparent obliviousness to any 'reality principle', is a much less sympathetic character than his sister but there is a kind of existential integrity in his insistence on the binding nature of their vows to each other. In murdering Annabella, he is simply fulfilling the terms of their betrothal: 'Love me or kill me, brother.'

In honour of the approaching feast, Soranzo had said that he would 'cause our lady / To deck herself in all her bridal robes' (V. ii. 10–11), so Annabella must be imagined as going to her death in a white wedding dress. This images her innocence ('Go

thou white in thy soul') and strongly suggests a romantic mar-
riage-in-death more 'real' than the official 'holy rites' which we
never see actually performed. It is possible to stage the murder
so that it re-creates the tender formality of their betrothal as they
kneel, hold hands and kiss. The language at this point is dignified but deeply moving:

> Kiss me; if ever after-times should hear
> Of our fast-knit affections, though perhaps
> The laws of conscience and of civil use
> May justly blame us, yet when they but know
> Our loves, that love will wipe away that rigour,
> Which would in other incests be abhorr'd.
>
> (V. v. 68–73)

In Griffi's film the mutuality of the *Liebestod* is emphasised, as
Annabella bares her breast to the dagger and they clasp the handle together as they had done at their betrothal. However, the
words Ford gives to Annabella ('Will you be gone?', 'What
means this?', 'Brother unkind, unkind') are far from suggesting
a mutual decision to die and Giovanni's erotic tenderness is soon
transformed into the exultant and egotistical savagery of the
Senecan avenger:

> Thus die, and die by *me* and by *my* hand.
> Revenge is *mine*; honour doth love command.
>
> (V. v. 85–6, my italics)

At this moment he resembles Vindice ('"Tis I, 'tis Vindice, 'tis I')
more than Romeo. The blood splashes which would appear on
her white wedding dress could, in their implied mingling of the
carnal with the spiritual, help to signify a doomed romanticism,
but the total impact is more horrific and disturbing than this. As
mentioned earlier, more than one death is involved:

> The hapless fruit
> That in her womb receiv'd its life from me
> Hath had from me a cradle and a grave.
>
> (V. v. 94–6)

Whether or not a director chooses to draw attention to the horror of this, the fact remains that it is more as a crazed solipsist than as a devoted lover that Giovanni goes to act his 'last and greater part'.

'Trimm'd in reeking blood' and with Annabella's heart upon his dagger, he bursts in upon Soranzo's birthday feast as a Senecan extremist, glorying in his ability to outreach his adversary and exceed all previous limits in his revenge. As in the endings of *The Spanish Tragedy* and *Titus Andronicus*, there is some delay before the characters onstage can grasp the enormity of what is happening, and it is not until Vasques has returned from viewing the body of Annabella (fifty lines after Giovanni's first appearance) that they fully credit his wild boasts. The long delay in their reaction allows the offstage audience time to work through their own shocked response and come to terms with some of the implications. The heart on the dagger is the kind of extreme spectacle which critics of Renaissance drama usually hasten to justify in symbolic terms. Such moments are rendered less threatening if they can be allegorised or shown to conform to previous patterns of verbal imagery. Certainly there is no shortage of possible significance in this instance. Petrarchan hyperboles about possessing the heart of one's beloved (the heart conceived as the seat of the passions and the centre of the self) mingle with connotations of religious martyrdom and reminders of the eviscerations practised in public executions for treason. Any intended 'meaning' on the part of Giovanni may well conflict with the overall impression the spectator receives, as in *Julius Caesar*, where Brutus tries to make a murder look like a sacrifice by getting the conspirators to bathe their arms in Caesar's blood, but only succeeds in making them look like butchers. In his Preface to *The Picture of Dorian Gray*, Wilde wrote that: 'All art is at once surface and symbol. Those who go beneath the surface do so at their peril. Those who read the symbol do so at their peril.'[16] The dripping heart on Giovanni's dagger is, as Michael Neill has eloquently argued, simultaneously overloaded with symbolic meaning and disconcertingly literal:

Vasques' sarcastic incomprehension ('What strange riddle's this?' l. 29) is understandable; for the effect of this proliferation of metaphoric suggestion, this layering of riddle upon riddle, is finally to defeat the exegesis it seems to invite. The greater the load of alternative meanings heaped upon it, the more the heart seems to assert its atrocious physicality, driving a wedge between sign and signification, word and thing.[17]

Staged in the way that Queen Henrietta's Men would have originally staged it, with a pig's or sheep's heart being used rather than any more obviously artificial property, the spectacle can evoke a primal horror which exceeds any possibility of allegorisation. If this seems too impersonal a feeling to be classified as 'emotional depth', I would also argue that Giovanni's gesture enacts a basic psychological truth, one that D. H. Lawrence struggled often to express. The romantic absolutism which strives for a total merging of identity, 'to be ever one, / One soul, one flesh, one love, one heart, one all', can be a narcissistic desire for domination, for a complete possession which annihilates the otherness of the other person and leaves the victorious ego celebrating a meaningless triumph. As Giovanni clutches the bleeding heart, he thinks he possesses Annabella, but in fact he is left in a world of his own. The final horrific tableau carries much of the play's 'general significance and emotional depth'.

9

Perkin Warbeck

The full Quarto title of Ford's last major play reads *The Chronicle History of Perkin Warbeck: A Strange Truth*. However, it was entered in the Stationers' Register as 'a Tragedy called Perkin Warbecke'. It is often tempting to dismiss concern with genre as a form of neoclassical pedantry obsessed with irrelevant 'rules', but a number of major modern theorists, as varied as Mikhail Bakhtin, Northrop Frye and E. D. Hirsch, have powerfully restated the central importance of genre in literary theory. Bakhtin, arguing against the Russian Formalists' narrow emphasis on language, wrote that: 'Poetics should really begin with genre, not end with it. For genre is the typical form of the whole work, the whole utterance. A work is only real in the form of a definite genre.'[1] Rather than conceiving of genres as absolute transcendent forms, one should recognise in them the inescapably social and transactional nature of art. They help to establish a relationship between writer and audience, to create a horizon of expectations which will help to determine the significance of what is presented. The 'meaning' of a literary work cannot be derived from its words and sentences alone but from the 'total utterance' of its publication or performance in a particular context.

In the case of Renaissance plays we know that it was the theatrical custom for the stage to be hung with black for the performance of a tragedy, but there has been little critical discussion of the difference which the presence (or absence) of such a generic marker would make in borderline cases like *Richard II* or *Perkin Warbeck*. An audience convinced by the black hangings that it was watching a tragedy would presumably be more inclined to look on Perkin as the emotional and dramatic centre of the play which bears his name, whereas the absence of such a cue might encourage a more historical and political reading of the play's events, one which threw the emphasis more on the astuteness of Henry VII than on the pity owing to the counterfeit king. Brief reflection upon this well-documented playhouse practice produces some further intriguing (and unanswerable) questions. Who would have been responsible for the decision to signal that the play was a tragedy by hanging the stage with black? Would it necessarily have been the author? Would the operative criteria have been political as well as aesthetic (since the degree of tragic sympathy encouraged for a pretender to the English throne was obviously a politically sensitive matter)? Was tragedy the only genre which it was possible to signal in this way?

This last question is important because in the absence of any indication to respond to *Perkin Warbeck* as a tragedy, 'chronicle history' is not the only alternative form which might help to shape the audience's expectations. The Quarto's subtitle *A Strange Truth* draws attention to the romance element in Ford's play. The word 'strange' echoes through Shakespeare's last plays and the appropriate emotional response to their 'strange but true' events is wonder rather than terror or pity.[2] The captured Perkin is presented to Henry as 'the Christian world's strange wonder' (V. ii. 36) and there are many suggestions of fairytale or romance material in this story of a man who claims to be a prince brought up in secret after being miraculously saved from death when a little child. However ironically intended, the Countess of Crawford's reference to Perkin's followers as 'disguised princes, / Brought up, it seems, to honest trades' (II. i. 13–14) associates them with numerous romantic narratives (such as Lacey's stratagem in *The Shoemaker's Holiday*). Huntly's disgusted comment on the wedding celebrations for Perkin and his daughter ('And all this for King Oberon and Queen Mab' – III. ii. 11) has a similar effect. Mary Shelley's three-volume novel *The*

Fortunes of Perkin Warbeck (1830) was subtitled *A Romance* and Ford's play can be seen as dramatising the way romance turns to tragedy when it encounters the 'real' world of history and politics.

We do not know enough about the original staging of *Perkin Warbeck* to decide which genre (if any) was given primary emphasis and hence what sort of 'contract' Ford established with his audience. Modern critical decisions about what kind of play Ford wrote tend to present themselves as the outcome of detailed analysis of its constituent parts rather than as the controlling framework for such an analysis, but they remain haunted by the paradox of the 'hermeneutic circle' (whereby the whole can only be determined by reference to the parts while the parts can only be determined by reference to the whole). As throughout the previous chapters, I shall be arguing that evidence which derives from the experience of the play in the theatre should be given particular weight, and so I will be making extensive reference to the one professional revival which has taken place in the twentieth century, the RSC production directed by John Barton and Barry Kyle at the Other Place in 1975.

In this production, some of the problems with Perkin as a tragic protagonist became very obvious and, to the surprise of many critics, Henry emerged as the true centre of dramatic interest.[3] According to the *Sunday Telegraph* reviewer, 'the central figure of Warbeck is totally overshadowed by the chuckling, human portrayal of the English King by Tony Church, a masterly performance against which Terence Wilton's brave imposter has little chance of survival, or even interest, in his lost cause'.[4] Similarly, G. K. Hunter wrote that, 'in comparison with Mr Church both Stuart Wilson (as James IV of Scotland) and Terence Wilton (as Perkin) seemed cardboard cut-outs of royalty'.[5] It could be argued that the whole style of the production was designed to achieve this more political and historical emphasis. Rather than the stage being hung with black, it was designed as a giant chessboard and surrounded with portraits of kings, genealogical diagrams and a map of the battle of Bosworth. Perkin, dressed all in white, appeared romantically glamorous but ineffectual when confronted with this crushing weight of history, whilst Henry, using a spotlight from time to time to point out some of the figures on the walls, seemed energetically and intelligently in

control of events. In response to this production, it seems necessary to re-examine not only the kind of dramatic and emotional
engagement which the play seeks from its audience but also the
more specific question of its original political significance.

Both Anne Barton and Philip Edwards have linked *Perkin Warbeck* with another 'pretender' play of the early 1630s, Massinger's
Believe as You List (1631), and argued that the two works are intended to comment critically on Charles I's style of government:

> Both resurrect the myth of the hero who returns from the dead
> to save his oppressed people, and they do so in ways which
> suggest, delicately, that their real subject is England under
> the rule of Charles I. These nostalgic and conservative plays
> use Henry VII and Flaminius, Massinger's representative of
> Rome, to personify what seemed at the time to be the danger-
> ous innovation and autocracy of Charles's rule. Standing
> against these politicians, and doomed to lose, is a king figure
> of another and more traditional kind: a man who not only 'has
> a kind of beauty of being', but who 'is the guardian of the
> idealized, authentic, undivided life, when truth and govern-
> ment were not separated'.[6]

This argument seems much more convincing to me when
applied to *Believe as You List* than to *Perkin Warbeck*. Massinger's
play, one of his best, had originally told the story of one of the
various claimants to be Sebastian, King of Portugal, believed
killed at the battle of Alcacer-el-Kebir in 1578 shortly before the
annexation of Portugal by Spain. The peace treaty Charles had
signed with Spain in November 1630 made the censor nervous
of anything which might disturb the new international order and
Massinger was forced to relocate his story in classical times.
However, the new Prologue, with delightful disingenuousness,
seems to provoke the audience into looking for topical applica-
tions:

> yf you finde what's Roman here,
> *Grecian*, or *Asiaticqe*, drawe to nere
> a late, & sad example, tis confest
> hee's but an English scoller at his best,
> a stranger to Cosmographie, and may erre

in cuntries names, the shape, & character
of the person he presents. . .

The 'late, & sad example' to which the play may 'drawe to nere'
was undoubtedly Frederick of Bohemia, Charles's brother-in-law,
left with no hope of recovering his kingdom by this latest turn
in English foreign policy. Massinger is unambiguous in his presentation of Antiochus as the true King of Lower Asia, tragically
thwarted, like Frederick, by 'necessitie of state'.

Ford's play may also have worried the censor since there is an
intriguing phrase in the Stationers' Register entry about 'observ-
ing the Caution in the License'. Moreover, there is an obvious
link with the 1630s in the fact that it is the Spanish ambassador
Hialas who persuades James, in the interests of a European
peace, to cease championing Perkin. However, despite his many
noble qualities, Perkin remains a pretender rather than a true
claimant, and one who shows little sign of being able to govern
effectively should he achieve a throne. It is difficult to see him as
the hero of a topical allegory in the way that Antiochus is intended to be, and nor is he a convincing embodiment of a
traditional kingliness to set against the rapacious extra-parlia-
mentary manoeuvrings of Charles I. As Verna Foster has put it,

if Perkin Warbeck is to be seen as offering a reproach to the
government of Charles I . . . the reproach surely lies not in the
ineffectual Perkin as the glamorous evocation of an earlier and
better style of monarchy, but rather in the competence of
Henry VII, which his descendant might do well to emulate.[7]

Francis Bacon had in fact dedicated his *History of the Reign of
Henry VII* (1622), one of Ford's principle sources for *Perkin
Warbeck*, to the then Prince Charles, and although Bacon is sometimes critical of Henry's behaviour he succeeds in giving the heir
to the throne a vivid picture of the first Tudor's powerful competence. Ford's Henry is also a very subtle portrait in which a
tough, unillusioned pragmatism seems to be combined with
more tender feelings, though in such a way as to leave one
uncertain whether the expression of these feelings is not itself
part of a calculated policy. As head of state, he is content to 'let
justice / Proceed in execution' on the traitor Stanley but he also

expresses personal grief for 'The loss of one whom I esteem'd a
friend' (II. ii. 41). This mixture of firmness and pity makes precisely the right impression on his assembled lords:

> SURREY: 'Tis a king
>   Compos'd of gentleness.
> DURHAM: Rare and unheard of;
>   But every man is nearest to himself,
>   And that the king observes; 'tis fit 'a should.
>   (II. ii. 49–52)

It is 'fit' that a monarch, whatever his finer feelings, should have
no illusions about the fact that every man is essentially out for
himself. That this last observation comes from a bishop, adds
force (as well as irony) to the commendation.

Henry's obsession with money, emphasised in the RSC production by having him clutch a portable treasure chest and
account book, might remind one of the permanent financial difficulties of the later Stuarts, but the crucial and deliberately
signalled distinction is that Henry's zeal to tax his subjects remains within constitutional bounds:

> We'll not abate one penny what in parliament
> Hath freely been contributed; we must not;
> Money gives soul to action.
>   (III. i. 27–9)

If Henry can be accused of appearing at times like a chartered
accountant, he cannot be accused, like Charles, of seeking to impose subsidies on his people without the consent of Parliament,
and nor does any 'undeserving favourite . . . boast / His issues
from [his] treasury' (IV. iv. 50–1). His rule may be 'politic' but it
is neither wilful nor autocratic.

Henry is not Charles and in fact the closer resemblance, with
hindsight at any rate, is that between Perkin and Charles. The
'royal actor' of Marvell's 'Horatian Ode' looked like a king and
could die like a king, but could not govern like one. Sealed off
from apprehending the reality of his situation by 'a total conviction of his own rectitude',[8] he came to look more and more like
Ford's tragic pretender and ended by sharing his 'martyrdom of

majesty'. The critically fashionable emphasis on the essential
theatricality of royal power, the way it seeks to maintain itself
through shows and representations, finds only limited endorsement in *Perkin Warbeck*. It is indeed possible to see all of Henry's
words and actions as conforming to a carefully controlled public
persona, but the play also makes a clear distinction between the
'shadow of majesty' and the substance of effective rule. Henry
may be able to manipulate the inflow of information about Perkin's movements so as to create the cunning impression of
almost supernatural foresight but it remains indisputably true
that 'with him / Attempts and execution are one act' (IV. iv. 67–
8). Perkin can dismiss Henry's right to the throne as deriving
merely from his victory at Bosworth but he cannot shake his
occupancy of that throne since 'The same arts that did gain / A
power must it maintain.' However much Perkin might look like
a king, when his own Bosworth beckoned he 'fled without battle
given' (V. i. 58).

By virtue of its subject-matter, *Perkin Warbeck* is inescapably a
political play but it does not seem primarily designed to comment directly on contemporary politics in the manner of *Believe
as You List*, though it may lend itself to a number of possible ap-
plications. What interested Ford in Perkin's story was probably
the chance it offered to build a play round a classic opposition
of personalities, in the manner of Shakespeare's *Richard II* or
Chapman's Byron plays. In Shakespeare and Chapman a self-
contained, inscrutable and 'politic' winner faces a more eloquent,
theatrical and emotionally extreme loser. Moral and political
judgements are complicated by the way Richard and Byron,
whatever their faults, become centres of tragic interest. Bolingbroke's sardonic refusal to be impressed by the figure strutting
and fretting before him is echoed by Henry's response to Perkin's defiant eloquence:

> O, let him range.
> The player's on the stage still, 'tis his part;
> 'A does but act.
>   (V. ii. 67–9)

In an earlier scene, the Bishop of Durham had said contemptuously of the traitor Stanley, 'Give losers leave to talk; / His loss

is irrecoverable' (II. ii. 95–6) and it is something of a critical commonplace that in the tragedies of Shakespeare and his contemporaries it is usually the eloquent suffering of life's losers that is the chief source of dramatic interest rather than the political acumen of their successful adversaries. What the revival of *Perkin Warbeck* seemed to show, however, was that Henry was actually more interesting as well as more successful than Perkin, and that Ford, as so often, had developed a stock situation in a new way.

A little reflection confirms that Henry has a much bigger range of moods and tones of voice than the pretender. At various points in the piay he is calculating, aggressive, self-satisfied, ironic, shocked, grief-stricken, merciful, jovial and courtly. By contrast, Perkin tends to speak in a rather undifferentiated, slightly stiff and abstract manner which remains within quite a narrow emotional range. The failure of Perkin to upstage Henry in the way that Richard upstages Bolingbroke takes us to the heart of the special dramatic problem posed by Ford's treatment of the story. What the Revels editor has called Ford's 'masterstroke of invention . . . the real stroke of genius, which makes the whole thing worthwhile' (in other words, Ford's decision to omit any admission by Perkin that he is an impostor) may be paradoxically a source of weakness as well as strength.[9] The unblinking fixity with which Perkin adheres to his assumed identity makes normal kinds of character development or emotional fluctuation impossible. What we are left with is an unusual variant of the problem of the Stoic tragic protagonist discussed in chapter 7.

Perkin of course is not a Stoic (at one point he is even described as 'effeminately dolent [sorrowful]') but his absolute and constant commitment to a conception of self which is at odds with general perception has something of the fiercely maintained autonomy of the Stoic wise man:

> Who to himself is law, no law doth need,
> Offends no King, and is a King indeed.
> (Chapman, *Bussy D'Ambois*, II. i. 203–4)

When Perkin speaks of 'How constantly my resolution suffer'd / A martyrdom of majesty!' (V. iii. 75–6), we are reminded of the frequency with which 'constancy' and 'resolution' figure as key terms in Ford's broadly Stoic moral pamphlets, *The Golden Meane* and *A Line of Life*. The dramatic problem involved is most neatly expressed in Perkin's line to his wife: 'But I am perfect sweet, I fear no change . . .' (IV. iii. 125). He will neither change, nor develop, nor permit us any glimpse of a self at odds with his chosen role.

This means that the investigation and questioning of identity in *Perkin Warbeck* is, despite the promising nature of the basic story, rather less thoroughgoing than in some other tragedies of the period. The Italian Neoplatonists had eloquently celebrated man's Protean capacity to transform himself into whatever he wished to become. God tells Adam in Pico della Mirandola's *Oration on the Dignity of Man* (1486) that 'We have made thee neither of heaven nor of earth, neither mortal nor immortal, so that with freedom of choice and with honor, as though the maker and molder of thyself, thou mayest fashion thyself in whatever shape thou shalt prefer.'[10] If Perkin's career is to be viewed positively as an example of this sort of 'Renaissance self-fashioning', then a fully effective dramatisation of his existential choice would require a scene of transformation like the thrilling moment when Tamburlaine discards his lowly shepherd's clothes to don full armour. However, Perkin arrives on the stage with his new identity already firmly fixed and 'Protean' is the last word one would associate with him.

Much more common in Renaissance tragedy than the celebration of man's power to act any part he chooses is the close scrutiny of characters whose sense of identity is challenged to the point of breakdown. When Richard II loses his crown, he is thrown into an existential crisis, becoming 'nothing':

> I have no name, no title –
> No, not that name was given me at the font –
> But 'tis usurped.
>
> (IV. i. 255–7)

He proceeds to act out this disintegration by smashing the mirror held up to his face, provoking an interchange with Bolingbroke about the extent to which all this is merely 'acting'. Even when a sense of self is with great difficulty maintained, as in the case

of the Duchess of Malfi, the severity of the challenge opens up a
gap between character and role which inevitably generates reflections on existence as an empty and oppressive charade:

> I account this world a tedious theatre,
> For I do play a part in't 'gainst my will.
>
> (IV. i. 83–4)

The point is that a theatrically interesting examination of identity
normally requires some kind of gap between self and mask to
become visible, or at least for a void beneath the mask to be
detectable. The effectiveness of Pirandello's *Henry IV*, the way it
is able to play so compellingly with reality, illusion, sanity and
madness, depends on it including a breakdown of the protagonist's delusory belief that he is an eleventh-century Holy Roman
Emperor, a breakdown which shatters the collective pretence he
has forced those around him to maintain: 'And you are amazed
that I tear off their ridiculous masks now, just as if it wasn't I
who had made them mask themselves to satisfy this taste of
mine for playing the madman.'[11] In *Perkin Warbeck*, however, the
mask never slips for a moment. The assumed identity is welded
on so perfectly that we can glimpse nothing behind it.

Surprisingly, it is the pragmatic politician Henry, rather than
the romantic pretender Perkin, who suffers the most serious and
dramatic challenge to his sense of self. His great opening speech
('Still to be haunted, still to be pursued . . .') begins by complaining that the Yorkist pretenders have come close to making him a
'mockery king' and ends by characterising the continued threat
to his reign in significantly absolute and existential terms: 'Ourself is scarce secure' (I. i. 14).[12] Throughout the rest of this first
scene Henry aggressively reasserts himself, aided by a chorus of
supporting nobles, but the real moment of crisis comes in the
third scene, with the news of Stanley's treachery. The change of
scene from a crowded open court to the privacy of Henry's
chamber in the Tower at dead of night seems to mark a movement inward towards the private man behind the public figure.
The disloyalty of Henry's closest friend and confidant rocks the
foundations of his being more dramatically than anything that
happens to Perkin:

Sir William Stanley? Who? Sir William Stanley?
My chamberlain, my counsellor, the love,
The pleasure of my court, my bosom friend,
The charge and the controlment of my person,
The keys and secrets of my treasury,
The all of all I am! I am unhappy:
Misery of confidence! – Let me turn traitor
To mine own person, yield my sceptre up
To Edward's sister and her bastard duke!

(I. iii. 104–12)

The strong indications of a psychological as well as a political
crisis ('The all of all I am! . . . Let me turn traitor / To mine own
person') are not surprising since it was Stanley who had actually
placed the crown on Henry's head at Bosworth, conferring his
new identity upon him in an improvised ritual as dramatic as his
parody of the baptismal gesture which brands Clifford with 'a
state-informer's character'. Ford was unable to depict directly
the moment at Bosworth but he does provide some visual con-
firmation of Stanley's importance by making him one of the two
nobles by whom Henry is *supported to his throne* in the opening
scene. With this prop removed, Henry is forced to question who
he is; Perkin never does and there is no comparable inward
movement taking us closer to the man behind the mask. How
close we really do get to Henry remains a matter of dispute since
his grief and shock involve a degree of self-dramatisation reminiscent of Richard II demonstrating with his mirror 'How soon
my sorrow hath destroyed my face.' On receipt of the news of
Stanley's betrayal, Henry demands that a torch be held up to
him: 'Urswick, the light! / View well my face, sirs; is there blood
left in it?' (I. iii. 87–8). For all the theatrical self-consciousness of
this, there seems little doubt, however, that we are witnessing a
real crisis of identity, as of course we are in the deposition scene
of *Richard II*, despite the evident histrionics of Richard.

The one moment when Perkin's assumed identity seems seriously threatened passes quickly enough on the printed page but
was staged with great emphasis by the RSC so as to recall these
other moments of selfhood in jeopardy. Perkin's emotional reaction to the ebbing of his fortunes at the Scottish court causes his
supporter Frion to say:

> You grow too wild in passion; if you will
> Appear a prince indeed, confine your will
> To moderation.
>
> (IV. ii. 20–2)

At Stratford, Frion accompanied this rebuke by holding a mirror up to Perkin's face. The dangerous word 'appear', with or without any accompanying gesture, sets off a further storm in the pretender which has the intensity of a patient's last desperate resistance to the uncovering of long-repressed traumatic material:

> What a saucy rudeness
> Prompts this distrust! If I will appear?
> Appear a prince? Death throttle such deceits
> Even in their birth of utterance! cursed cozenage
> Of trust! Ye make me mad; 'twere best, it seems,
> That I should turn impostor to myself,
> Be mine own counterfeit . . .
>
> (IV. ii. 22-8)

The RSC used a lighting change at this point to throw Perkin's shadow on the wall, capturing and mocking his frantic gesticulations and recalling a similar change of lighting when the torch was held to Henry's face.[13] But the crisis is quickly over and Perkin is once again 'perfect' in his role, unreachable by argument, persuasion or threat.

The consequent inability of Ford to dramatise anything of his protagonist's inner life makes it difficult for an audience to experience the kind of emotional engagement characteristic of tragedy. Henry had said of Stanley, 'But I could see no more into his heart / Than what his outward actions did present' (II. ii. 31–2) and the audience is placed in a similar position with regard to Perkin. Reviewing the Stratford production for the *Birmingham Post*, Keith Brace wrote that, 'It is almost Brechtian, if that word still has any meaning, in its refusal to allow the spectator to commit his allegiance to any of the characters. . . . Yet what we long for, spoiled by Shakespeare, is pathos in the role of Warbeck, and that Ford does not give us.'[14] In fact, the word 'pity' occurs frequently in Ford's play but the peculiarity of Perkin's situation makes it uncertain what kind of pity is appropriate, the conventional tragic pity for a fallen prince or the different kind of pity one feels for a madman. In telling his 'story of a prince's ruin', Perkin presents himself to the Scottish court as 'A subject of the rarest kind of pity / That hath in any age touch'd noble hearts' (II. i. 42–3). When he is later brought as a prisoner to the English court, he is no longer a ruined prince but only 'a shadow / Of majesty'. This, however, has the effect of making him 'a substance / Of pity' (V. ii. 33–4). The initial compassionate reaction which he provokes in Katherine and the other Scottish ladies seems a curious compound of both kinds of pity:

> Beshrew me, but his words have touch'd me home,
> As if his cause concern'd me. I should pity him
> If 'a should prove another than he seems.
>
> (II. i. 118–20)

Since his noble demeanour and tragic tale have already strongly moved her, it is unclear whether the last sentence means that she would pity him *even if* he were to prove other than he seems or *especially if* he were to be exposed as a fraud or madman. A similar uncertainty of response afflicts the audience, leaving in suspension the different possible ways of relating emotionally to his predicament. Only the final humiliation in the stocks seems designed to make that most radical moral demand – to pity suffering, whoever suffers and for whatever cause.

As a stage emblem, the spectacle of Perkin in the stocks retains a certain ambiguity. There was an allegorical tradition, evident in a number of Tudor interludes, of depicting Justice, Truth or other virtues being placed in the stocks, and Shakespeare probably had this in mind when he showed Kent suffering this fate in *King Lear*.[15] On the other hand, one might equally call to mind the way the *pretensions* to righteousness of Overdo, Busy and Wasp are similarly punished in *Bartholomew Fair*. Rather than pushing us towards a final judgement on Perkin, the last scene demands only that we pity his suffering and admire his courage. He would probably be dressed in rags, perhaps bearing visible signs of the tortures which historically were inflicted on him, and there are poignant hints of Christ's Passion in the mockery of this self-styled 'King'. In the Stratford production, Perkin was clad in a sheet marked 'Richard IV', quietly

paralleling the sign 'King of the Jews' under which Christ suf-
fered. The emotional distance which Ford's method of presenting
Perkin inevitably entailed is bridged in this last scene by the
presence of his wife Katherine, whose loyalty leads her, dressed
'in her richest attire' as she was in the previous scene, to share
willingly in her husband's public humiliation. When told to
'come from that impudent impostor', her reply is powerful and
moving:

> You abuse us;
> For when the holy churchman join'd our hands,
> Our vows were real then; the ceremony
> Was not in apparition but in act. –
> Be what these people term thee, I am certain
> Thou art my husband.
>   (V. iii. 113–18)

Katherine's fidelity represents Perkin's one great moral victory
over Henry, whose own wife is never seen and whose closest
friend betrayed him. The question of Perkin's 'truth' comes to
seem less important than his wife's 'troth' and their parting kiss
gives the final scene its emotional centre. More even than
Penthea, Calantha, Annabella, Giovanni or Perkin himself, Katherine embodies the values Ford chose to identify himself with in
the anagram of his own name which appears on the title pages
of four of his plays (including this one) – 'Fide Honor'.

Notes

1 Revivals, Reputations and the Question of Value

1. This objection was made even in relation to the tragedies of Shakespeare: 'Lady Macbeth is a barbarian, whom we must remove centuries from us before we can admit the psychological sufficiency of ambition to account for her homicidal career. Of Othello's action, too, we feel that gentlemen "don't do that sort of thing" in our times' (S. P. Sherman, 'Forde's Contribution to the Decadence of the Drama', in *John Fordes Dramatische Werke*, ed. W. Bang [Louvain: A. Uystpruyst, 1908] p. xiv).

2. 'Notes on London at the End of the War', in *Europe without Baedeker* (1967), quoted in *John Webster*, ed. G. K. and S. K. Hunter (Harmondsworth: Penguin, 1969) p. 150.

3. *Roscius Anglicanus*, quoted in *Webster: The Critical Heritage*, ed. Don D. Moore (London: Routledge, 1981) p. 5.

4. Quoted in Moore, *Webster: The Critical Heritage*, p. 36.

5. Charles Lamb, *Specimens of English Dramatic Poets who Lived about the Time of Shakespeare* (1808; London: George Bell, 1897) p. iii.

6. Ibid.

7. William Hazlitt, 'On Reason and Imagination', in *The Plain Speaker* (1826), vol. XII of *The Complete Works*, ed. P. P. Howe (London: J. M. Dent, 1931) p. 53.

8. A. C. Swinburne, 'John Webster', in *The Age of Shakespeare*, vol. XI of *The Complete Works*, ed. Edmund Gosse and T. J. Wise (London: Heinemann, 1926) p. 281.

9. Lamb, *Specimens of English Dramatic Poets*, p. 228. Havelock Ellis's remark occurs in his Introduction to the Mermaid edition of Ford's plays (1888; London: Benn, 1960) p. xvi.

10. Inside front cover of *Sight and Sound* (April 1993). In fact, despite adding a number of horrors to Ford's ending, Guiseppe Patroni Griffi's

film is more remarkable for its beautiful photography than for any 'decadent' extremism.

11. William Archer, *The Old Drama and the New* (1924), quoted in Moore, *Webster: The Critical Heritage*, p. 143.

12. Edmund Gosse, *The Jacobean Poets* (1894), quoted in Moore, *Webster: The Critical Heritage*, p. 152.

13. T. S. Eliot, 'Ben Jonson', in *Selected Essays*, 3rd edn (London: Faber, 1951) p. 155.

14. Ibid., p. 159.

15. There still remains a perceived risk in putting on anything non-Shakespearean. In 1991, the Sheffield Crucible planned to present *The Revenger's Tragedy* as part of its autumn season but 'in the light of the current economic climate' replaced it at the last minute with *As You Like It*. Their artistic director Mark Brickman argued that 'all the indications suggest a fairly chilly autumn, and frankly we'd be taking a bit of a flyer with a play which doesn't really exist in the public's consciousness' (*Guardian*, 12 July 1991).

16. Tony Richardson, 'Why We Revived *The Changeling*', *Plays and Players* (1961), quoted in Wendy Griswold, *Renaissance Revivals: City Comedy and Revenge Tragedy in the London Theatre, 1576–1980* (Chicago: University of Chicago Press, 1986) p. 171. The other reasons Richardson gave were 'the extraordinary existentialism of the theme' and Middleton's 'understanding of a certain kind of sexual violence, an almost Strindbergian love–hatred relationship'.

17. Susan Sontag, 'Against Interpretation', in *A Susan Sontag Reader*, intr. Elizabeth Hardwick (Harmondsworth: Penguin, 1983) p. 104.

18. Norman Rabkin, *Shakespeare and the Problem of Meaning* (Chicago: University of Chicago Press, 1981) p. 19.

19. Ibid., pp. 22–3.

20. Ibid., p. 27.

21. Jonathan Dollimore, *Radical Tragedy: Religion, Ideology and Power in the Drama of Shakespeare and his Contemporaries* (Brighton: Harvester, 1984) p. 192. Dollimore is speaking with reference to *King Lear*. For a contrary view, see T. McAlindon, 'Tragedy, *King Lear*, and the Politics of the Heart', *Shakespeare Survey*, vol. XLIV (1992) 85-90.

22. Martin Hoyle, *The Times* (24 May 1993). The piece was performed at the Chelsea Theatre Centre and directed by Andy Lavender.

23. Sontag, 'Against Interpretation', p. 99.

24. *The Theatre and Its Double*, in *Artaud on Theatre*, ed. Claude Schumacher (London: Methuen, 1989) p. 116.

25. Brook talking about his production of the *Marat/Sade* in an interview with the *Daily Mail* (26 August 1964), quoted in Sally Beauman, *The Royal Shakespeare Company: A History of Ten Decades* (Oxford: Oxford University Press, 1982).

26. William Blake, 'The Human Abstract', in *Songs of Experience*, in *The Complete Poems*, ed. Alicia Ostriker (Harmondsworth: Penguin, 1977). The counterpart in *Songs of Innocence* is 'The Divine Image'.

27. Emmanuel Levinas, 'Ethics as First Philosophy', in *The Levinas Reader*, ed. Sean Hand (Oxford: Blackwell, 1989) p. 83.

28. Jackson's letter is quoted in *The Riverside Shakespeare*, ed. G. Blakemore Evans *et al.* (Boston, Mass: Harvard University Press, 1974) appendix B, no. 33, p. 1852 (though it did not appear in the original printing of this edition but was silently added at a later date).

29. Peter Hall has said, 'I don't believe you can do these Greek plays without masks. In tragedy, the emotion is so strong it needs the containment of the mask' (interview with Michael Billington, *Guardian*, 28 May 1993).

30. George Steiner, *Real Presences* (London: Faber, 1989) p. 144.

31. Northrop Frye, 'Violence and Television', in *Reading the World: Selected Writings, 1935–76*, ed. Robert D. Denham (New York: Peter Lang, 1990) p. 371.

32. Primo Levi, *The Drowned and the Saved*, trans. Raymond Rosenthal (London: Abacus [Sphere Books], 1989) pp. 39–40.

2 Webster and Jacobean Theatre

1. The phrase Milton was to use about his own literary ambitions. See the Preface to Book II of *The Reason of Church Government* (1641), in John Milton, *Selected Prose*, ed. C. A. Patrides (Harmondsworth: Penguin, 1974).

2. Henry Fitzjeffrey, 'Notes from Blackfriars', quoted in *Webster: The Critical Heritage*, ed. Don D. Moore (London: Routledge, 1981).

3. *London's Dove* (1612), quoted in the footnote to IV. ii. 173 by J. R. Brown in the Revels Plays edition of *The Duchess of Malfi*.

4. This gap in Webster's career would be partially filled if it could be conclusively demonstrated that a manuscript fragment of an early seventeenth-century tragedy dealing with Alessandro de' Medici, Duke of Florence, was indeed the work of Webster, as was claimed by the auction house which put it up for sale in 1986. See Richard Proudfoot, 'A Jacobean Dramatic Fragment', *The Times Literary Supplement* (13 June 1986) p. 651, and subsequent correspondence. There is a very full, scholarly survey of the evidence in Anthony Hammond and Doreen Delvecchio, 'The Melbourne Manuscript and John Webster: A Reproduction and Transcript', *Studies in Bibliography*, vol. XLI (1988) 1–32.

5. A reliable one-volume history of the period is Derek Hirst, *Authority and Conflict: England 1603–1658* (London: Arnold, 1986; repr. with corrections, 1987). Reflections on some of the controversial developments in Stuart historiography can be found in Simon Adams, 'Early Stuart Politics: Revisionism and After', in *Theatre and Government under the Early Stuarts*, ed. J. R. Mulryne and Margaret Shewring (Cambridge: Cambridge University Press, 1993) pp. 29–56.

6. I have pursued this argument further in 'Jacobean Pageant or Elizabethan Fin-de-Siècle? The Political Context of Early Seventeenth-Century Tragedy', in *Jacobean Drama as Social Criticism*, ed. James Hogg (New York: Edwin Mellen, 1994).

7. Fulke Greville, *A Dedication to Sir Philip Sidney* (usually known as *The Life of Sir Philip Sidney*), in *The Prose Works of Fulke Greville, Lord Brooke*, ed. John Gouws (Oxford: Clarendon Press, 1986) p. 135.

8. A number of books have examined the literary consequences of this Calvinist dominance. See John Carey, *John Donne: Life, Mind and Art* (London: Faber, 1981); Alan Sinfield, *Literature in Protestant England 1560–1660* (London: Croom Helm, 1983); John Stachniewski, *The Persecutory Imagination: English Puritanism and the Literature of Religious Despair* (Oxford: Clarendon Press, 1991).

9. Quoted (in translation) in Stachniewski, *The Persecutory Imagination*, p. 220.

3 The White Devil

1. Emrys Jones, in *The Times Literary Supplement*, 28 June 1991, p. 17.

2. John Webster, 'Sit in a full Theater, and you will thinke you see so many lines drawne from the circumference of so many eares, whiles the *Actor* is the *Center*' ('An excellent Actor', in *The Complete Works of John Webster*, ed. F. L. Lucas [London: Chatto, 1927] vol. IV, p. 42). This was one of thirty-two 'Characters' added by Webster to the sixth edition (1615) of the collection attributed to Sir Thomas Overbury.

3. Lucas, *The Complete Works of John Webster*, vol. I, p. 27.

4. Catherine Belsey, *The Subject of Tragedy: Identity and Difference in Renaissance Drama* (London: Methuen, 1985) pp. 160–4.

5. See J. R. Brown's Revels Plays edition, pp. lx–lxi.

6. Heidegger discusses the significance of death within the framework of his existential philosophy in sections 46–53 of *Being and Time*, trans. John Macquarrie and Edward Robinson (Oxford: Blackwell, 1962).

7. T. McAlindon, *English Renaissance Tragedy* (Basingstoke: Macmillan, 1986) p. 153.

8. Montaigne, *The Essayes of Michael Lord of Montaigne*, trans. John Florio (1603), ed. Henry Morley (London: Routledge, 1885) lxviii, pp. 26–7.

9. Thomas Tuke, *A Discourse of Death* (London: G. Norton, 1613) p. 26.

10. Montaigne, *Essayes*, lxviii, p. 26.

4 The Duchess of Malfi

1. In Shakespeare's play, Caesar corresponds to the phlegmatic type, Brutus to the melancholic, Cassius to the choleric, and Antony to the sanguine. For a detailed argument relating this characterisation to an overall symbolic design, see T. McAlindon, *Shakespeare's Tragic Cosmos* (Cambridge: Cambridge University Press, 1991) ch. 4.

2. Michael Billington, *Guardian*, 6 July 1985.

3. *La Duchesse de Malfi*, adapted by Claude Duneton and directed by Matthias Langhoff, at the Theatre de la Ville, Paris. Reviewed in *The Times Literary Supplement*, 24 May 1991, p. 19.

4. Primo Levi, *The Drowned and the Saved*, trans. Raymond Rosenthal (London: Abacus [Sphere Books], 1989) ch. 3, 'The Grey Zone', p. 36.

5. Ibid., p. 39.

6. Northrop Frye, *Anatomy of Criticism: Four Essays* (Princeton, NJ: Princeton University Press, 1957) p. 219.

7. Lisa Jardine, *Still Harping on Daughters: Women and Drama in the Age of Shakespeare* (Brighton: Harvester, 1983) p. 72.

8. Ibid., p. 77.

9. Keith Sturgess, *Jacobean Private Theatre* (London: Routledge, 1986) p. 114. Although I disagree with Sturgess's emphasis here, I think his chapter on *The Duchess of Malfi* is generally excellent.

10. T. S. Eliot, *The Waste Land*, ll. 377–81 in *Collected Poems 1909–1962* (London: Faber, 1974). Webster's hold on Eliot's imagination was such that the bedchamber scene may actually be a source for these lines. In Act IV, the numerous suggestions of a marriage ritual make it almost certain that Webster intended the Duchess to go to her death with her hair loose and flowing like a bride's.

11. I have discussed this topic, and its relevance to *The Duchess of Malfi*, more fully in *Suicide and Despair in the Jacobean Drama* (Brighton: Harvester, 1986).

12. Milton, *Paradise Lost*, IV. 505–8, in Milton, *Poetical Works*, ed. D. Bush (London: Oxford University Press, 1966).

13. John Foxe, *Acts and Monuments*, 4th edn (London: John Day, 1583) p. 1422.

14. Emmanuel Levinas, 'Useless Suffering', trans. Richard Cohen, in *The Provocation of Levinas: Rethinking the Other*, ed. R. Bernasconi and D. Wood (London: Routledge, 1988) pp. 158–67.

15. Paul Taylor, *Independent*, 9 December 1989.

16. Charles Osborne, *Daily Telegraph*, 11 December 1989.

17. The single surviving copy of this engraving is not the original but a reworked version dating from after 1633. Births and deaths subsequent to the first printing have resulted in a number of changes and James himself now holds a skull. For more detailed descriptions, see Bernard M. Wagner, 'New Verses by John Webster', *Modern Language Notes*, vol. XLVI (1931) pp. 403–5, and Charles Forker, *Skull Beneath the Skin: The Achievement of John Webster* (Carbondale and Edwardsville: Southern Illinois University Press, 1986) pp. 169–70.

18. Michael Billington, *Guardian*, 6 July 1985.

5 *The Devil's Law-Case*

1. John Donne, Elegie II, 'The Anagram', ll. 15–16, in *The Complete English Poems of John Donne*, ed. C. A. Patrides (London: Dent, 1985).

2. The fullest discussion of Renaissance tragicomedy in relation to Webster is Jacqueline Pearson, *Tragedy and Tragicomedy in the Plays of John Webster* (Manchester: Manchester University Press, 1980).

3. *The Dramatic Works in the Beaumont and Fletcher Canon*, gen. ed. Fredson T. Bowers, vol. III, p. 497.

4. From Abraham Wright's *Commonplace Book* (*c.*1650), reprinted in *Webster: The Critical Heritage*, ed. Don D. Moore (London: Routledge, 1981) p. 35.

5. The ambiguity of this encounter is expressed through a curious slippage of meaning in the word 'Italian'. Contarino first speaks, in character, of he and Ercole living or dying together 'like noble gentlemen, / And true Italians' (II. i. 297–8) before adding, in a manner which reflects English prejudices rather than his own perspective, 'Methinks, being an Italian, I trust you / To come somewhat too near me' (II. i. 299–300).

6. Most of the relevant details can be found in Lucas's introduction and notes to *The Devil's Law-Case* (in vol. II of *The Works of John Webster*) or in Akiko Kusunoki, 'A Study of *The Devil's Law-Case*: with Special Reference to the Controversy over Women', *Shakespeare Studies (Tokyo)*, vol. XXI (1982–3) 1–33.

7. Anthony Weldon, *The Court and Character of King James* (1650), quoted in Kusunoki, 'A Study of *The Devil's Law-Case*', p. 5.

8. Quotations from letters dated 20 February 1619, 25 January 1620 and 12 February 1620, in vol. II of *The Letters of John Chamberlain*, ed. N. E. McClure (Philadelphia: The American Philosophical Society, 1939).

9. The title page of the 1623 edition describes it as having been 'Acted by her Majesties Servants'. Queen Anne died on 2 March 1619.

10. Nicholas de Jongh, *Guardian*, 7 June 1980. John Barber, for the *Daily Telegraph*, agreed that 'Annette Kerr's matron was too groomed and wholesome' (10 June 1980) but Ned Chaillet in *The Times* enjoyed 'the clarity of Miss Kerr's matronly pose' (9 June 1980).

11. For John Barber, the play was 'immensely worth seeing' (*Daily Telegraph*, 10 June 1980). Nicholas de Jongh thought it 'exciting to see how a forgotten piece came to life on stage' (*Guardian*, 7 June 1980) and Ned Chaillet wrote that if the reputation of the play grew, 'this production will be the main reason' (*The Times*, 9 June 1980).

12. Thomas Nashe, *Pierce Penniless his Supplication to the Devil*, in *The Unfortunate Traveller and Other Works*, ed. J. B. Steane (Harmondsworth: Penguin, 1972) pp. 74–5.

13. These include the play's two most recent editors, D. C. Gunby and Elizabeth Brennan.

14. Sir Thomas Browne, *Religio Medici*, section 9, in Sir Thomas Browne, *The Major Works*, ed. C. A. Patrides (Harmondsworth: Penguin, 1977) p. 69.

6 Ford and Caroline Theatre

1. See, for instance, vol. IV of *The Revels History of Drama in English*, ed. Philip Edwards *et al.* (London: Methuen, 1981); Martin Butler, *Theatre and Crisis 1632–42* (Cambridge: Cambridge University Press, 1984); Kevin Sharpe, *Criticism and Compliment: The Politics of Literature in the England of Charles I* (Cambridge: Cambridge University Press, 1987); and

Keith Sturgess, *Jacobean Private Theatre* (London: Routledge, 1986), which, despite its title, covers the Caroline period as well.

2. From a poem written in 1630 to accompany the publication of Davenant's *The Just Italian*. Quoted in Andrew Gurr, 'Ford and Contemporary Theatrical Fashion', in *John Ford: Critical Revisions*, ed. Michael Neill (Cambridge: Cambridge University Press, 1988) p. 86.

3. Volume III of *The Plays and Poems of Philip Massinger*, ed. Philip Edwards and Colin Gibson, 5 vols (Oxford: Clarendon Press, 1976).

4. John Dryden, 'Of Dramatic Poesy: An Essay', in *Selected Criticism*, ed. James Kinsley and George Parfitt (Oxford: Clarendon Press, 1970) p. 70. Neander is the speaker.

5. Martin Butler, '*Love's Sacrifice*: Ford's Metatheatrical Tragedy', in Neill, *John Ford: Critical Revisions*, pp. 201–31.

6. Umberto Eco, *Reflections on 'The Name of the Rose'*, trans. William Weaver (London: Secker and Warburg, 1985) pp. 67–8.

7. It is possible that Ford was responsible for a lost play called *A Bad Beginning Makes a Good Ending*, which was acted by the King's Men at court during the Christmas season of 1612–13. In 1660 the bookseller Humphrey Moseley attributed three comedies to Ford which have subsequently been lost. These were *The Royal Combat*, *The London Merchant* and a play referred to prolixly as *An Ill Beginning Has a Good End, and a Bad Beginning May Have a Good End*. It is quite probable that the last of these was the same play which was acted in 1612–13, but Moseley's attributions have frequently turned out to be unreliable and it remains a little unlikely that a first play by a new dramatist should have been selected for court performance.

8. 'In honorable memory of the Right noble the Earle of Devonshire *late deceased*' (l. 41), in *The Nondramatic Works of John Ford*, ed. L. E. Stock *et al.* (Binghampton, New York, 1991) p. 337.

9. Julia Gasper, *The Dragon and the Dove: The Plays of Thomas Dekker* (Oxford: Clarendon Press, 1990) pp. 190–217. Detecting topical allusions in *The Sun's Darling* is complicated by the fact that the surviving text includes revisions made for a court performance in 1638–9.

10. *Annals of English Drama 975–1700*, ed. A. Harbage (rev. S. Schoenbaum), 3rd ed. rev. Sylvia Wagonheim (London: Routledge, 1989).

11. 'These two marks of the modern mind – belief in scientific determinism and faith in extreme individualism – will serve to identify Ford with modern thought' (G. F. Sensabaugh, *The Tragic Muse of John Ford* [Stanford: Stanford University Press, 1944] p. 10).

12. For a full account of this quarrel, see Andrew Gurr, 'Ford and Contemporary Theatrical Fashion', in Neill, *John Ford: Critical Revisions*, pp. 81–96.

13. Clifford Leech, *John Ford and the Drama of his Time* (London: Chatto, 1957) p. 122.

14. Ibid., p. 122.

15. Butler, *Theatre and Crisis*; Albert H. Tricomi, *Anticourt Drama in England 1603–1642* (Charlottesville: University of Virginia Press, 1989).

16. A very different view of Ford, placing him within a 'Catholic

coterie', is advanced by Lisa Hopkins in *John Ford's Political Theatre* (Manchester: Manchester University Press, 1994), which appeared after I had completed my book.

17. From *Histrio-Mastix*, quoted in vol. IV of *The Revels History of Drama in English*, p. 64.

18. Charles Lamb, *Specimens of English Dramatic Poets* (1808; London: George Bell, 1897) p. 228.

7 The Broken Heart

1. *Spectator* (20 July 1962), quoted in Roger Warren, 'Ford in Performance', in *John Ford: Critical Revisions*, ed. Michael Neill (Cambridge: Cambridge University Press, 1988) p. 11. *The Times* (10 July 1962) p. 13 (given incorrectly as 11 July 1962 in T. J. B. Spencer's Revels Plays edition). My book went to press before Michael Boyd's production of *The Broken Heart* opened at the Swan in October 1994.

2. Clifford Leech, *John Ford*, British Council Pamphlet (Harlow: Longman, 1964) p. 30.

3. Harriet Hawkins, 'Mortality, Morality, and Modernity in *The Broken Heart*: Some Dramatic and Critical Counter-arguments', in Neill, *John Ford: Critical Revisions*, p. 147.

4. Charles Lamb, *Specimens of English Dramatic Poets* (1808; London: George Bell, 1897) p. 228.

5. *The Times* reviewer was greatly impressed by Rosemary Harris as Penthea ('It is in itself a good acting part and one could hope for few better interpreters'), less so by Joan Greenwood as Calantha ('Some may find Miss Joan Greenwood's Calantha too mannered a performance, for all its dignity and strength'). A third centre of emotional interest, one less easy for a reader to detect, was created by Olivier's powerful performance as Bassanes: 'In the hands of Sir Laurence, Bassanes . . . is raised to almost excessive authority. . . . The tortured wisdom of Bassanes, like the waste of Penthea, is tragic. At these two points we are no longer watching a dated ritual' (*The Times*, 10 July 1962, p. 13).

6. Sigmund Freud, 'Mourning and Melancholia', trans. James Strachey, in vol. XI of *The Pelican Freud Library*, ed. Angela Richards (Harmondsworth: Penguin, 1984) pp. 251–68 (p. 254).

7. Ibid., p. 257.

8. Quoted in T. J. B. Spencer (ed.), *The Broken Heart* (Manchester: Manchester University Press, 1980) p. 13.

9. *The Times* (10 July 1962) p. 13. The sentence quoted was in reference to the whole play rather than just the penultimate scene. In fact, the review appeared under the heading 'Ritual Admired from a Distance'.

10. *John Ford*, ed. Havelock Ellis (1888; London: Ernest Benn, 1960) p. xvi.

11. Clifford Leech, *John Ford and the Drama of his Time* (Manchester: Manchester University Press, 1980) pp. 72 and 74. Ronald Huebert writes at length on Ford's relation to baroque painting and sculpture in

John Ford: Baroque English Dramatist (Montreal: McGill-Queen's University Press, 1977).

12. Walter Pater, *The Renaissance: Studies in Art and Poetry* (1873; London: Macmillan, 1913) p. 135. A number of important twentieth-century critics, such as Northrop Frye and Susanne Langer, have followed Pater in seeing music as the type of all the arts.

13. Nietzsche, *The Birth of Tragedy* (1872), trans. Shaun Whiteside, ed. Michael Tanner (Harmondsworth: Penguin, 1993) p. 35.

14. Ibid., p. 103.

15. Ibid., p. 80.

16. Ford, *The Golden Meane*, in *The Nondramatic Works of John Ford*, ed. L. E. Stock *et al.* (Binghampton, New York, 1991) p. 246.

17. Sigmund Freud, *Beyond the Pleasure Principle*, trans. James Strachey, in vol. XI of *The Pelican Freud Library*, pp. 275–338.

8 *'Tis Pity She's a Whore*

1. Introduction to *'Tis Pity She's a Whore*, ed. Derek Roper, p. lv. 'Jacobean' is not a loose usage or slip of the pen since Roper considers that *'Tis Pity* 'may have been written at virtually any time before 1633. . . . It may quite easily have been a Jacobean play in fact as well as spirit' (p. xli).

2. T. S. Eliot, 'John Ford', in *Selected Essays*, 3rd edn (London: Faber, 1951) p. 198.

3. Charles Dibdin, *A Complete History of the English Stage*, quoted in an appendix to the Revels Plays edition, p. 133.

4. See Lévi-Strauss, *Structural Anthropology* (1958), trans. Claire Jacobson and Brooke Grundfest Schoepf (London: Allen Lane, 1968).

5. Cyrus Hoy, '"Ignorance in Knowledge": Marlowe's Faustus and Ford's Giovanni', *Modern Philology*, vol. LVII, no. 3 (February 1960) 145–54.

6. I have restored the 1633 Quarto's capitalisations of 'Deity', 'Hell', and 'Nature' which Sturgess puts into lower case. The initial capitals seem more appropriate in the context of this kind of metaphysical argument.

7. John Donne, *Biathanatos*, ed. Michael Rudick and M. Pabst Battin (New York: Garland, 1982) I. i. 7, p. 54.

8. Hugo Grotius, *Of the Law of Warre and Peace* (1625), trans. C. Barksdale (1655), quoted in Robert Ornstein, *The Moral Vision of Jacobean Tragedy* (Madison: University of Wisconsin Press, 1960) p. 207.

9. Irving Wardle, *The Times*, 4 August 1972.

10. *Stratford Herald*, 29 July 1977.

11. Alan C. Dessen, '*'Tis Pity She's a Whore*: Modern Productions and the Scholar', in *'Concord in Discord': The Plays of John Ford 1586–1986*, ed. Donald K. Anderson (New York: AMS Press, 1986) p. 93.

12. *Observer*, 28 February 1988.

13. Roger Holdsworth, reviewing the Swan production, thought that '[Jonathan] Cullen's volatile neurotic, torn between tenderness, exul-

tation, and despair, is probably the best way of explaining [Giovanni's] extraordinary switches of thought and tone' (*The Times Literary Supplement*, (5 July 1991).

14. Marlowe, Sestiad II, ll. 287–8, in *The Poems*, ed. Millar Maclure (London: Methuen, 1968).

15. Claire Armitstead (*Guardian*, 12 May 1992), reviewing the play after its transfer to the Pit.

16. Oscar Wilde, *Plays, Prose Writings and Poems* (London: J. M. Dent, 1990) pp. 63–4.

17. Michael Neill, '"What Strange Riddle's This?": Deciphering *'Tis Pity She's a Whore'*, in *John Ford: Critical Revisions*, ed. Michael Neill (Cambridge: Cambridge University Press, 1988) p. 163.

9 Perkin Warbeck

1. P. N. Medvedev and Mikhail Bakhtin, *The Formal Method in Literary Scholarship*, trans. A. J. Wehrle (Baltimore: Johns Hopkins University Press, 1978) p. 129. See also Northrop Frye, *Anatomy of Criticism: Four Essays* (Princeton, NJ: Princeton University Press, 1957) and E. D. Hirsch, *Validity in Interpretation* (New Haven, Conn.: Yale University Press, 1967).

2. The distinction I am making may not have seemed so clearcut to Renaissance theorists. Sidney speaks of tragedy as 'stirring the affects of admiration [i.e. wonder] and commiseration' (*An Apology for Poetry*, ed. Geoffrey Shepherd [Manchester: Manchester University Press, 1973] p. 118). In Shepherd's note to this passage, he says that, 'For Sidney, admiration is a kind of emotional shock, the amazement felt in the face of an exceptionally heroic order of behaviour. In thus replacing Aristotle's terror by admiration Sidney avoids the difficulty of having to explain how the contemplation of horror can be an instructive or delightful process' (p. 190).

3. See Verna Ann Foster's excellent article, 'Perkin without the Pretender: Reexamining the Dramatic Center of Ford's Play', *Renaissance Drama*, n.s. vol. XVI (1985) 141–58.

4. *Sunday Telegraph*, 10 August 1975.

5. G. K. Hunter, *Research Opportunities in Renaissance Drama*, vol. XVIII (1975) p. 60.

6. Anne Barton, 'He that Plays the King: *Perkin Warbeck* and the Stuart History Play', in *English Drama: Forms and Development*, ed. Marie Axton and Raymond Williams (Cambridge: Cambridge University Press, 1977) pp. 80–1. Barton in this passage is summarising, quoting and agreeing with Philip Edwards, 'The Royal Pretenders: Ford's *Perkin Warbeck* and Massinger's *Believe As You List*', the first version of which appeared in *Essays and Studies* (1974). Lisa Hopkins, in *John Ford's Political Theatre* (Manchester: Manchester University Press, 1994) takes this reading of the play further by arguing for a belief within Ford's circle that Perkin really was Richard, Duke of York.

7. Foster, '*Perkin* without the Pretender', p. 157.

8. Derek Hirst, *Authority and Conflict: England 1603–1658* (London: Arnold, 1986; repr. with corrections, 1987) p. 137.

9. Introduction to *Perkin Warbeck*, Revels edn, ed. Peter Ure (London: Methuen, 1968) pp. xli and xlii.

10. Mirandola, *De Hominis Dignitate*, trans. Elizabeth Forbes, in *The Renaissance Philosophy of Man*, ed. Ernst Cassirer *et al.* (Chicago: Chicago University Press, 1956) p. 225.

11. Luigi Pirandello, *Henry IV*, in *Naked Masks: Five Plays by Luigi Pirandello*, ed. Eric Bentley (New York: E. P. Dutton, 1952) p. 189.

12. Sturgess has 'Oneself' but this appears to be a misprint rather than a deliberate emendation of the Quarto's 'Ourself'. In my next quotation I have also departed slightly from Sturgess, restoring a missing definite article before 'controlment' (I. iii. 107).

13. See Roger Warren, 'Ford in Performance', in *John Ford: Critical Revisions*, ed. Michael Neill (Cambridge: Cambridge University Press, 1988) pp. 23–4.

14. *Birmingham Post*, 8 August 1975.

15. See T. W. Craik, *The Tudor Interlude* (Leicester: Leicester University Press, 1958) pp. 93-5. Referring to a German woodcut of 1525 showing Justice imprisoned in the stocks by Usury and Tyranny, Craik wrote that 'the fact that Flettner's picture was re-engraved as late as 1647 testifies to the continuing life of the tradition' (p. 95).

Bibliography

Editions Used

Webster

Quotations from *The White Devil*, *The Duchess of Malfi* and *The Devil's Law-Case* are taken from D. C. Gunby (ed.), *John Webster: Three Plays* (Harmondsworth: Penguin, 1972). Fuller annotations can be found in the following important editions of the individual plays:

J. R. Brown (ed.), *The White Devil*, The Revels Plays (London: Methuen, 1960).
J. R. Brown (ed.), *The Duchess of Malfi*, The Revels Plays (London: Methuen, 1964).
Elizabeth M. Brennan (ed.), *The Devil's Law-Case*, The New Mermaids (London: Benn, 1975).

In addition to these, Kathleen McLuskie and Jennifer Uglow have edited a valuable 'performance text' of *The Duchess of Malfi* (Bristol: Bristol Classical Press, 1989). Other works of Webster, except for the collaborations with Dekker which can be found in the Bowers edition of Dekker's plays, are quoted from F. L. Lucas (ed.), *The Complete Works of John Webster*, 4 vols (London: Chatto, 1927).

Ford

Quotations from *The Broken Heart*, *'Tis Pity She's a Whore* and *Perkin Warbeck* are taken from Keith Sturgess (ed.), *John Ford: Three Plays*

(Harmondsworth: Penguin, 1970; repr. 1985). As in the case of Webster, there are very fully annotated editions of the individual plays:

T. J. B. Spencer (ed.), *The Broken Heart*, The Revels Plays (Manchester: Manchester University Press, 1980).

Derek Roper (ed.), *'Tis Pity She's a Whore*, The Revels Plays (London: Methuen, 1975).

Peter Ure (ed.), *Perkin Warbeck*, The Revels Plays (London: Methuen, 1968).

Love's Sacrifice, The Fancies Chaste and Noble and *The Lady's Trial* are quoted from William Gifford (ed.), *The Works of John Ford*, 3 vols, rev. Alexander Dyce (1869; repr. New York: Russell and Russell, 1965). The remaining plays are quoted in the following editions:

R. F. Hill (ed.), *The Lover's Melancholy*, The Revels Plays (Manchester: Manchester University Press, 1985).

W. Bang (ed.), *The Queen, or the Excellency of her Sex* (Louvain: A. Uystpruyst, 1906).

The Dekker collaborations can be found in Bowers, with the exception of *The Spanish Gypsy* which is printed in A. H. Bullen's edition of *The Works of Middleton*, 8 vols (London: John Nimmo, 1885–6). Ford's other writings are quoted from L. E. Stock *et al.* (eds), *The Nondramatic Works of John Ford* (Binghampton, New York, 1991).

Other dramatists

Anon. [Middleton?], *The Revenger's Tragedy*, in *Thomas Middleton: Five Plays*, ed. B. Loughrey and N. Taylor (Harmondsworth: Penguin, 1988).

Beaumont, Francis and John Fletcher, *The Dramatic Works in the Beaumont and Fletcher Canon*, gen. ed. Fredson T. Bowers, 8 vols to date (Cambridge: Cambridge University Press, 1966–).

Chapman, George, *Bussy D'Ambois*, ed. Nicholas Brooke, The Revels Plays (London: Methuen, 1964).

Dekker, Thomas, *The Dramatic Works of Thomas Dekker*, ed. Fredson T. Bowers, 4 vols (Cambridge: Cambridge University Press, 1953–61).

Jonson, Ben, *Ben Jonson*, ed. C. H. Herford and Percy and Evelyn Simpson, 11 vols (Oxford: Clarendon Press, 1925-52).

Kyd, Thomas, *The Spanish Tragedy*, ed. Philip Edwards, The Revels Plays (London: Methuen, 1959).

Marlowe, Christopher, *Doctor Faustus*, ed. Roma Gill, The New Mermaids, 2nd edn (now based on the A Text) (London: Black, 1989).

Marston, John, *The Malcontent*, ed. G. K. Hunter, The Revels Plays (London: Methuen, 1975).

Massinger, Philip, *The Plays and Poems of Philip Massinger*, ed. Philip Edwards and Colin Gibson, 5 vols (Oxford: Clarendon Press, 1976).
Middleton, Thomas, *Thomas Middleton: Five Plays*, ed. B. Loughrey and N. Taylor (Harmondsworth: Penguin, 1988).
Shakespeare, William, *The Complete Pelican Shakespeare*, gen. ed. Alfred Harbage, rev. ed. (Baltimore: Penguin; London: Allen Lane, 1969).
Tourneur, Cyril, *The Atheist's Tragedy*, ed. Irving Ribner, The Revels Plays (London: Methuen, 1964).

Select Bibliography of Other Works

Anderson, D. K., *John Ford* (New York: Twayne, 1972).
Anderson, D. K. (ed.), *'Concord in Discord': The Plays of John Ford 1586–1986* (New York: AMS Press, 1986).
Barroll, J. Leeds *et al.* (eds), *The Revels History of Drama in English*, vol. III: *1576–1613* (London: Methuen, 1975).
Barton, Anne, 'He that Plays the King: Perkin Warbeck and the Stuart History Play', in Marie Axton and Raymond Williams (eds), *English Drama: Forms and Development* (Cambridge: Cambridge University Press, 1977) pp. 69–93.
Belsey, Catherine, *The Subject of Tragedy* (London: Methuen,1985).
Berry, Ralph, *The Art of John Webster* (Oxford: Clarendon Press, 1972).
Bliss, Lee, *The World's Perspective: John Webster and the Jacobean Drama* (New Brunswick, NJ: Rutgers University Press, 1983).
Bogard, Travis, *The Tragic Satire of John Webster* (Berkeley: University of California Press, 1955).
Bradbrook, M. C., *John Webster: Citizen and Dramatist* (London: Weidenfeld, 1980).
Braden, Gordon, *Renaissance Tragedy and the Senecan Tradition* (New Haven, Conn.: Yale University Press, 1985).
Braunmuller, A. R. and Michael Hattaway (eds), *The Cambridge Companion to English Renaissance Drama* (Cambridge: Cambridge University Press, 1990).
Briggs, Julia, *This Stage-Play World: English Literature and its Background 1580–1625* (Oxford: Oxford University Press, 1983).
Brooke, Nicholas, *Horrid Laughter in Jacobean Tragedy* (London: Open Books, 1979).
Brown, J. R. and Bernard Harris (eds), *Jacobean Theatre* (London: Arnold, 1960; repr. with corrections, 1965).
Butler, Martin, *Theatre and Crisis 1632–1642* (Cambridge: Cambridge University Press, 1984).
Callaghan, Dympna, *Woman and Gender in Renaissance Tragedy* (Hemel Hempstead: Harvester, 1989).
Cave, Richard Allen, *'The White Devil' and 'The Duchess of Malfi': Text and Performance* (Basingstoke: Macmillan, 1988).
Champion, Larry, *Tragic Patterns in Jacobean and Caroline Drama* (Knoxville: University of Tennessee Press, 1977).

Clare, Janet, *'Art Made Tongue-tied by Authority': Elizabethan and Jacobean Dramatic Censorship* (Manchester: Manchester University Press, 1990).

Cronin, Lisa, *Professional Productions in the British Isles since 1880 of Plays by Tudor and Early Stuart Dramatists: A Checklist* (University of Warwick, 1987).

Dessen, Alan, *Elizabethan Stage Conventions and Modern Interpreters* (Cambridge: Cambridge University Press, 1984).

Dollimore, Jonathan, *Radical Tragedy: Religion, Ideology and Power in the Drama of Shakespeare and his Contemporaries* (Brighton: Harvester, 1984).

Dutton, Richard, *Mastering the Revels: The Regulation and Censorship of English Drama* (Basingstoke: Macmillan, 1991).

Edmond, Mary, 'In Search of John Webster', *The Times Literary Supplement*, 24 December 1976, pp. 1621–2.

Edwards, Philip, 'The Royal Pretenders: Ford's *Perkin Warbeck* and Massinger's *Believe As You List*', in *Threshold of a Nation: A Study in English and Irish Drama* (Cambridge: Cambridge University Press, 1979).

Edwards, Philip *et al.* (eds), *The Revels History of Drama in English*, vol. IV: *1613–1660* (London: Methuen, 1981).

Eliot, T. S., *Selected Essays*, 3rd edn (London: Faber, 1951).

Ellis-Fermor, Una, *The Jacobean Drama*, 4th edn rev (London: Methuen, 1958).

Farr, Dorothy, *John Ford and the Caroline Theatre* (Basingstoke: Macmillan, 1979).

Felperin, Howard, *Shakespearean Representation: Mimesis and Modernity in Elizabethan Tragedy* (Princeton, NJ: Princeton University Press, 1977).

Ford, Boris (ed.), *The Age of Shakespeare*, *The New Pelican Guide to English Literature*, vol. II, rev. edn (Harmondsworth: Penguin, 1982).

Forker, Charles, *Skull Beneath the Skin: The Achievement of John Webster* (Carbondale and Edwardsville: Southern Illinois University Press, 1986).

Foster, Verna Ann, '*Perkin* without the Pretender: Reexamining the Dramatic Center of Ford's Play', *Renaissance Drama*, n.s. vol. XVI (1985) 141–58.

Griswold, Wendy, *Renaissance Revivals: City Comedy and Revenge Tragedy in the London Theatre, 1576–1980* (Chicago: University of Chicago Press, 1986).

Gunby, D. C., '*The Devil's Law-Case*: An Interpretation', *Modern Language Review*, vol. LXIII (1968) 545-58.

Gurr, Andrew, *Playgoing in Shakespeare's London* (Cambridge: Cambridge University Press, 1987).

Gurr, Andrew, *The Shakespearean Stage, 1574–1642*, 3rd edn (Cambridge: Cambridge University Press, 1992).

Hammond, Antony and Doreen Delvecchio, 'The Melbourne Manuscript and John Webster: A Reproduction and Transcript', *Studies in Bibliography*, vol. XLI (1988) 1–32.

Hirst, Derek, *Authority and Conflict: England 1603–1658* (London: Arnold, 1986; repr. with corrections, 1987).

Hogg, James (ed.), *Jacobean Drama as Social Criticism* (New York: Edwin Mellen, 1994).

Holdsworth, R. V. (ed.), *Webster: 'The White Devil' and 'The Duchess of Malfi': A Casebook* (Basingstoke: Macmillan, 1975).

Hopkins, Lisa, *John Ford's Political Theatre* (Manchester: Manchester University Press, 1994).

Huebert, Ronald, *John Ford: Baroque English Dramatist* (Montreal: McGill-Queen's University Press, 1977).

Hunter, G. K. and S. K. (eds), *John Webster* (Penguin Critical Anthologies) (Harmondsworth: Penguin, 1969).

Jardine, Lisa, *Still Harping on Daughters: Women and Drama in the Age of Shakespeare* (Brighton: Harvester, 1983).

Jensen, Ejner J., 'Lamb, Poel, and our Postwar Theatre: Elizabethan Revivals', *Renaissance Drama*, n.s. vol. IX (1978) 211–34.

Kaufmann, R. J., 'Ford's "Waste Land": *The Broken Heart*', *Renaissance Drama*, n.s. vol. III (1970) 167–87.

Kusunoki Akiko, 'A Study of *The Devil's Law-Case*: with Special Reference to the Controversy over Women', *Shakespeare Studies (Tokyo)*, vol. XXI (1982–3) 10–33.

Leech, Clifford, *John Webster* (London: Hogarth Press, 1951).

Leech, Clifford, *John Ford and the Drama of his Time* (London: Chatto, 1957).

Leech, Clifford, *John Ford*, British Council Pamphlet (Harlow: Longman, 1964).

Leggatt, Alexander, *Jacobean Public Theatre* (London: Routledge, 1992).

Lever, J. W., *The Tragedy of State* (London: Methuen, 1971).

Lockyer, Roger, *The Early Stuarts: A Political History of England 1603–1642* (London: Longman, 1989).

Luckyj, Christina, *A Winter's Snake: Dramatic Form in the Tragedies of John Webster* (Athens, Ga.: University of Georgia Press, 1989).

Lomax, Sarah, *Stage Images and Traditions: Shakespeare to Ford* (Cambridge: Cambridge University Press, 1987).

McAlindon, T., *English Renaissance Tragedy* (Basingstoke: Macmillan, 1986).

McLuskie, Kathleen, *Renaissance Dramatists*, Feminist Readings (Hemel Hempstead: Harvester, 1989).

Moore, Don D. (ed.), *Webster: The Critical Heritage* (London: Routledge, 1981).

Morris, Brian (ed.), *John Webster* (London: Benn, 1970).

Mulryne, J. R. and Margaret Shewring (eds), *Theatre and Government under the Early Stuarts* (Cambridge: Cambridge University Press, 1993).

Neill, Michael (ed.), *John Ford: Critical Revisions* (Cambridge: Cambridge University Press, 1988).

Oliver, H. J., *The Problem of John Ford* (Melbourne: Melbourne University Press, 1955).

Ornstein, Robert, *The Moral Vision of Jacobean Tragedy* (Madison: University of Wisconsin Press, 1960).

Pearson, Jacqueline, *Tragedy and Tragicomedy in the Plays of John Webster* (Manchester: Manchester University Press, 1980).

Potter, Lois, 'Realism Versus Nightmare: Problems of Staging *The Duchess of Malfi*', in Joseph G. Price (ed.), *The Triple Bond: Plays, Mainly Shakespearean, in Performance* (Pennsylvania: Pennsylvania State University Press, 1975).

Rabkin, Norman, *Shakespeare and the Problem of Meaning* (Chicago: University of Chicago Press, 1981).

Randall, Dale, *'Theatres of Greatness': A Revisionary View of Ford's 'Perkin Warbeck'* (Victoria, BC: University of Victoria, 1986).

Ribner, Irving, *Jacobean Tragedy: The Quest for Moral Order* (London: Methuen, 1962).

Ricks, Christopher (ed.), *English Drama to 1710*, rev. ed. (London: Sphere, 1987).

Sargeaunt, Pamela, *John Ford* (Oxford: Blackwell, 1935).

Sensabaugh, G. F., *The Tragic Muse of John Ford* (Stanford: Stanford University Press, 1944).

Sharpe, Kevin, *Criticism and Compliment: The Politics of Literature in the England of Charles I* (Cambridge: Cambridge University Press, 1987).

Sinfield, Alan, *Literature in Protestant England 1560–1660* (London: Croom Helm, 1983).

Stavig, Mark, *John Ford and the Traditional Moral Order* (Madison: University of Wisconsin Press, 1944).

Sturgess, Keith, *Jacobean Private Theatre* (London: Routledge, 1986).

Tricomi, Albert H., *Anticourt Drama in England 1603–1642* (Charlottesville: University of Virginia Press, 1989).

Ure, Peter, *Elizabethan and Jacobean Drama* (Liverpool: Liverpool University Press, 1974).

Wrightson, Keith, *English Society 1580–1680* (London: Heinemann, 1982).

Index